DISCUSSION PAPERS

I0616539

Heft 194

Ute Hippach-Schneider | Verena Schneider

Work-based learning in tertiary education in Europe – examples from six educational systems

Part II – case studies

Federal Institute for Vocational
Education and Training **BiBB** ▸

▸ Researching
▸ Advising
▸ Shaping the future

The ACADEMIC RESEARCH DISCUSSION PAPERS issued by the Federal Institute for Vocational Education and Training (BIBB) are published via the President. They appear in the form of signed contributions from their authors. The opinions expressed are those of the authors and do not necessarily reflect the views of the editor. They are subject to copyright. The purpose of publication is to engage in debate with the specialist academic research community.

Citation:
Hippach-Schneider, Ute; Schneider, Verena: Work-based learning in tertiary education in Europe – examples from six educational systems. Part II – case studies. Bonn 2018

1st edition 2018

Publisher:
Bundesinstitut für Berufsbildung, Bonn
Robert-Schuman-Platz 3
53175 Bonn
Internet: www.bibb.de

Publication management:
Stabsstelle „Publikationen und wissenschaftliche Informationsdienste"
E-Mail: publikationsmanagement@bibb.de
www.bibb.de/veroeffentlichungen

Production and distribution:
Verlag Barbara Budrich
Stauffenbergstraße 7
51379 Leverkusen
Internet: www.budrich.de
E-Mail: info@budrich.de

Licence:
The content of this work is subject to a Creative Commons Licence

 (licence type: Attribution – Non-Commercial – No Derivatives – 4.0 Germany). For further information, please visit our Creative Commons information site online at http://www.bibb.de/cc-lizenz.

ISBN 978-3-8474-2257-0 (Print)
ISBN 978-3-96208-085-3 (Open Access)

Order No. 14.194

Bibliographic information from the German National Library
The German National Library catalogues this publication in the German National Bibliography. Detailed information is available online at http://dnb.ddb.de.

Contents

Preface and introduction

As part of a research project in 2015/2016, the Federal Institute for Vocational Education and Training (BIBB) conducted a number of case studies to investigate models and functions of practice- or vocation-oriented training courses in the tertiary educational sector. The case studies relate to educational programmes in England, France, Ireland, Norway, Austria and Poland (https://www.bibb.de/de/24108.php).

BIBB already published structural analyses of the respective national tertiary educational sectors in the countries forming the object of comparison in 2016 (HIPPACH-SCHNEIDER and SCHNEIDER 2016). This new publication now evaluates the case studies themselves. In each case, we look at two national tertiary educational programmes which are characterised by specific practical orientation and frequently feature practical phases. For this purpose, interviews have been carried out with experts from the fields of educational policy and research, with representatives of education and training providers, with companies and with students themselves.

In overall terms, it is possible to say that all the states investigated are seeing developments in their tertiary educational sectors which may be summarised by using the term "vocationalisation". This vocationalisation is taking place via a new differentiation at the programme level, through the introduction of work-based learning elements and in the form of the upgrading of institutions from the vocational education and training (VET) sector of secondary education rather than primarily being reflected by the instigation of new educational establishments or governance structures.

The aim of the present publication is to help to create a deeper understanding of vocational or vocationally-oriented tertiary education which is individualised by the evaluations and experiences of the participants surveyed and by the various perspectives they display. Tertiary education is frequently still conflated with higher education or even with university education. This leaves so-called "higher vocational education and training" out of the equation. Tertiary vocational education and training in the wider sense of the term, a definition which also encompasses advanced vocational training and practice-integrated and practice-oriented higher education, is increasingly becoming a focus of educational policy since it provides an alternative to purely academic education and offers a high degree of potential for learners and for the diversity of educational systems as well as in terms of covering the needs of the labour market.

The paper begins by explaining the thematic background to the research project. This is followed by a description of the main project issues, of the theoretical approach adopted and of the methodology used.

The interview analyses of the case studies are then presented in two parts. Part 1 relates to the interviews conducted with representatives from the fields of educational policy, educational administration and educational research. The second part examines the interviews carried out with the students, companies and educational establishments.

1   Background

In vocational education and training as opposed to general or academic education, preparation for transition to the labour market is an identity-forming criterion which is inherent in the system. Such preparation may occur via full-time school-based training or via training within a dual VET model, but regardless of the form it takes the focus is always on the ability to exercise a qualified occupational activity directly after completion of training. There is a broad range of models within the international context. On the one hand, we have programmes which relate very closely to specific company tasks. By the same token, we also find programmes which impart broadly based employability skills and also include general content alongside specialist input.

The term "employability" has brought a particular dynamism to the higher education and academic debate with regard to this preparation function. Practice orientation and practice-based learning are now widespread in higher education programmes. This extends far beyond the fundamental understanding of bachelor's and master's degrees as well as the concept of binary higher education systems, but constitutes an additional specific subsector of professional and practice-based higher education.

This is achieved by elements such as mandatory practical placements or the dual structuring of educational programmes, some of which lead to double qualifications. There is also a variance in the nature and degree of formalisation of the cooperation agreements between the educational establishments and external partners such as companies or public administration bodies.

This form of expansion of vocational education and training, or of one of its basic characteristics, contrasts with the perception of a process of "academisation", something which is frequently borne out by rising numbers of graduates and participants in the tertiary sector. However, international statistics do not provide total transparency with regard to whether programmes have a "general" or "vocational" orientation. A further factor is that tertiary education extends beyond higher education. It is also the case that the numbers of participants in continuing and higher vocational training, which are very strong in some countries, are not fully mapped in international statistics (HIPPACH-SCHNEIDER 2014, HIPPACH-SCHNEIDER et al. 2017).

Consequently, there is a risk that the relevance of higher vocational training programmes for the national educational systems affected may be overlooked. This relevance particularly relates to the opportunity for further development, deepening and specialisation of professional competences after completion of initial vocational training and to the expansion of chances to access the university sector. Both functions of higher vocational education and training have an indirect effect on the attractiveness of initial vocational education and training because they open up prospects for different and multifarious educational pathways and professional careers. Discussion in Germany on achievement of the European benchmark that 40% of those aged between 30 and 34 should be in possession of a tertiary qualification by 2020 has, for example, solely centred on increasing the number of higher education qualifications. Raising the number of advanced vocational qualifications, which also form part of the tertiary sector, is an issue which has scarcely been addressed thus far.

Another issue which arises is the extent to which the adoption of characteristics of VET in higher education and university programmes has contributed to the growth of the higher education sector in Europe. These characteristics are not visible in the international statistics. Dual study models are registered as higher education rather than as vocational education and training. Greater visibility and a better understanding of higher education as vocational or vocationally-oriented education and training could help to reduce the stigma which often attaches to vocational education and training in the secondary sector.

2   Project objectives

The aim of the project was to make the relevance, the models and functions of the different forms of VET and work-based learning in the tertiary sector more visible in a multitude of ways.

> BIBB research project:
>
> "Work-based learning programmes in the tertiary educational sector – an international comparative analysis of models and functions (H–VET)", term I/2014 to III/2017
>
> More information available at https://www.bibb.de/de/24108.php

2.1   Qualitative interpretation of the international educational statistics

Tertiary education is a highly heterogeneous sector. It is often conflated with higher education. At the same time, international educational data collected on the basis of the so-called ISCED Classification (International Standard Classification of Education) also allocates educational programmes which take place outside higher education institutions to the tertiary sector.

Statistical data constitute an important decision-making foundation for evidence-based educational policy. Although the respective national data forms the initial object of focus, international statistics are required in order to analyse global developments and to be able to align the positioning of the individual country in worldwide comparative terms. As far as Europe is concerned, data is in particular provided by Eurostat (Statistical Office of the European Union). Data on the tertiary education sector is of relevance in terms of the question of increasing academisation versus *vocational drift* and with regard to the European benchmark relating to the proportion of those aged 30 to 34 who are in possession of a higher education qualification.

Following the revision of the ISCED Classification and the introduction of the 2011 version, no differentiated data is currently available which would permit the proportion of vocational or practice-oriented programmes in the tertiary sector to be identified. Indeed, it is up to individual states to decide whether they provide such differentiated data. Because of the highly varying approaches adopted, it is no longer possible to conduct cross-country comparisons.

This means that supplementary qualitative data is becoming more important to the visibility of vocational education and training. Such data shows whether vocational or practice-oriented programmes are on offer in the tertiary sector and what provision is available, e.g. advanced vocational education and training in Austria and Germany or practice-oriented higher education programmes.

The results of the project in respect of the visibility of vocational education and training and of vocational or practice-related higher education in the international educational statistics have already been published in sources such as the *Journal for Education and Training* and in an edited volume (Hippach-Schneider 2017, Hippach-Schneider et al. 2017). Attention was drawn to the fact that back-up qualitative research is needed in order to use this data as a basis for educational policy decisions if erroneous interpretations are to be avoided.

2.2   Analysis of the tertiary education sector

In order to improve understanding of which programmes are concealed behind the tertiary statistics, an investigation was undertaken within the scope of the project to identify which programmes have a vocational or practice-oriented alignment. This may relate to programmes which stipulate company-based phases of learning or mandatory practical placements (so-called work-based learning,[1] WBL) as well as to in-service programmes which require occupational experience and lead to a higher vocational qualification.

The central issues addressed within the country analyses were as follows:

▶ Which models of work-based learning or of higher vocational education and training programmes exist in the tertiary education and training sector in England, France, Ireland, Austria, Poland and Norway – the countries upon which the comparison is based?

▶ How are these programmes conceived and structured in terms of the following criteria:

  ▶ Structural (organisational) and curricular integration of learning university/college and business learning locations

  ▶ Role of businesses (cooperation partners of educational institutions, contractual partners of students)

  ▶ Scope of practice

  ▶ Organisation of learning in the business, e.g. are there guidelines for learning phases?

  ▶ Supervision of practical phases by university teachers and company (training) personnel.

▶ What are the functions of these education and training programmes in the education and training system?

▶ What are the common characteristics of the programmes which are attributed to the higher education sector?

▶ How do these differ from those outside the higher education sector?

These analyses were conducted in England, France, Ireland, Norway, Austria and Poland. The results of the system comparisons were published in 2016 in the academic research discussion paper "Tertiary vocational education and training in Europe – examples from six educational systems" (HIPPACH-SCHNEIDER and SCHNEIDER 2016).

2.3   Case studies of selected programmes

The analyses of the systems were supplemented by 12 case studies. Two programmes mainly from the areas of engineering/technology/information technology were chosen for each country on the basis of the results of the system analyses. Project teams together with national experts identified the personal experiences and assessments of the stakeholders involved. Five different perspectives were included. These encompassed the points of view of the educational

---

1 WBL is learning as part of programmes in which theoretical learning is connected with the observation of work processes in real workplaces and reflection on these work processes. The practical learning phases may be paid or unpaid. They may occur as part of differing institutional arrangements, for example as formalised *apprenticeships* or practical placements of varying duration. However, this does not include programmes in which practice-based learning takes place on shop floors, in workshops, learning companies or by means of simulation. In this respect, the understanding is more narrowly expressed than in the definition of CEDEFOP (2011).

establishment/teaching staff, the companies, students, policy makers and research. This publication presents the results of the evaluation of these case studies.

2.4   Theoretical approach

The theoretical approach adopted by the project links in with the theories propounded by Trow (1973, 2000, 2005) regarding the development of higher education systems and the influences of such systems on educational content.

Trow developed theories of educational expansion in the higher education sector as long ago as the 1970s. He differentiates between *elite, mass* and *universal higher education systems*. A system in which half or more of the population in the relevant age group participate in higher education is described as a universal higher education system. In a *mass higher education system*, this figure becomes 16 to 50 per cent. He defines a proportion of under 15 per cent as an elite system. Trow argues that the character of the institutions, the curricula and the pedagogy deployed all change during development from elite, to mass and to universal higher education systems. For example, the aim of elite systems to create a social elite would therefore be expressed in the curricula. These aim to mould the character and attitudes of the students via highly structured academic learning concepts. The institutions are small and homogeneous. There are clear barriers between the academic community and the rest of society. In contrast to this, the aim of the mass higher education system is to prepare a large segment of the population for a broad range of technical and economic managerial positions. The curricula are more modular and more flexible. Within the educational institutions, there is a larger range of different organisational structures and teaching areas. The barriers between the academic world and society are more open and permeable. The aim of universal systems is ultimately to prepare the entire population for social and technical change. The divisions between formally and informally acquired learning begin to disperse, as does the separation between educational institutions and other learning locations, such as the workplace. Trow regarded this typology as ideal types rather than as an empirical description of real systems. This makes it clear that the emergence of the next system type does not require complete disappearance of the previous system type. Trow's view is that this leads to the development of a mixture of elements (Trow 1973, 2000, 2005).

This theory arose in conjunction with an analysis of the consequences of educational expansion in the higher education sector and the development of categories of so-called "binary" or "unified" higher education systems. A higher education system is designated as being "binary" if it comprises two main groups. The second group in a binary system is frequently characterised by the fact that it offers vocational or semi-professional education, one example being the universities of applied sciences in Germany. In some cases such as in Ireland and Australia, these vocational institutions are "upgraded" and accorded university status, leading to the development of a "unified system".

Many higher education systems contain a mixture of educational establishments which differ with regard to prestige, resources and selectivity, with regard to specialisms and faculties, and with regard to students. One example of this is the US higher education system, which consists of high-prestige research universities, a second group of private and public four-year colleges and a large number of two-year colleges. Such a system is designated as being "diversified" (Teichler 2014).

The project was able to determine the extent to which WBL and higher vocational education and training models have led to a growing significance of vocational training elements in the tertiary sector which have not been reflected in new institutions or governance structures and thus would otherwise not be visible in some cases.

3 Evaluation of the case studies

This publication presents detailed evaluations of the case studies conducted. It provides a summary of current educational policy debate in the countries forming the object of comparison, focusing on developments at the time of the interviews conducted with representatives of ministries, public education administration and researchers as well as an analysis of personal experience of students, representatives of education institutions and companies with selected education programmes.

3.1 Methodological approach

As part of the case studies, guided interviews were conducted with stakeholders from the areas of vocational education and training, higher education and policymaking. Persons were interviewed both in their capacity as experts in their respective training system and also as representatives of specific vested interest groups whose role in and evaluations of the design and development process of the programmes we have sought to disclose. Five stakeholder groups were differentiated for the purpose of drawing up the guide. These were ministries/responsible authorities, students, researchers, educational establishments and companies. Appropriately tailored guides were used for each interview. A total of 63 interviews were conducted in the sample countries.[2]

Table 1: Summary of the educational programmes investigated

England	▶ Foundation Degree "Electrical and Electronic Engineering Programme" ▶ Higher Apprenticeship (Bachelor Programme) "WMG Applied Engineering Programme"
Ireland	▶ Advanced Certificate "Electrical Apprenticeship" (Further Education and Training) ▶ Higher Certificate "Information Technology Support Programme" (Higher Education)
Austria	▶ Dual Bachelor Study Programme "Smart Engineering of Production Technologies and Processes" ▶ Higher Vocational Qualification "Accountant Qualification"
France	▶ Diplôme Universitaire de Technologie (DUT) "Gestion des Entreprises et des Administrations" and Licence professionelle (LP) "Chargé de Clientèle" ▶ Brevet de Technicien Supérieur (BTS) "Banque"
Norway	▶ Bachelor Programme "Y-way" "Electrical Power Engineering" ▶ Programme at Technical College "Building and Construction"
Poland	▶ State School of Higher Professional Education "Mechanical Engineering" ▶ Two- and one-year programme in Learning Centre of New Technology "Electronics and Mechatronics"

Content structure qualitative analysis in accordance with KUCKARTZ (2014) was used for the evaluation of the interviews within the scope of the "H-VET" research project. This type of content analysis was selected for the H-VET research project because it affords the opportunity

---

2 Ten in England, 11 in France, 17 in Ireland, 11 in Norway, seven in Austria and seven in Poland.

to form new main and sub categories during the further course of the evaluation on the basis of the fundamental categories (developed from the interview guide) and on the basis of the interviews forming the object of analysis.

3.2   The educational policy and academic research perspective

3.2.1   England

In both Anglo-Saxon countries involved in the comparison there are clear indicators within educational policy as well as specific initiatives which point towards the strengthening and establishing of training programmes with a vocational and practical focus in the tertiary sector. This also particularly includes work-based models of learning in the form of *apprenticeships*.

Two developments characterise tertiary (higher) education in England. On the one hand, the United Kingdom[3] has one of the highest tertiary education participation rates in Europe. 47 per cent of those aged 30 to 34 have achieved at least a qualification at ISCED Level 5, compared with 39 per cent in the EU as a whole (Eurostat 2016). The latest figures show a higher education participation rate of 49% for persons aged up to 30. This statistic encompasses programmes in both the area of higher education and in the vocational education and training sector (DEPARTMENT FOR EDUCATION 2017). On the other hand, a sharp decline has been recorded in programmes at Level 5 of the European Qualifications Framework (EQF) (e.g. *HNCs= higher national certificates, HNDs= higher national diplomas, FDs = foundation degrees*). This development has mainly taken place in favour of qualifications at the higher levels of the EQF (WOLF/ DOMINGUEZ-REIG et al. 2016). Between 2011/12 and 2015/16, the number of registrations for bachelor courses of study rose by 1.5%. During the same period, a fall of 55% was recorded for programmes under bachelor level (mainly at EQF Level 5). This means that the latter now account for only just under eight per cent of all programmes below bachelor level (HIGHER EDUCATION STATISTICS AGENCY 2017).[4] Structural adjustments over recent years suggest the course is set for further growth in higher level academic qualifications.

As a consequence, the debate surrounding the higher education sector is focused on the issue of whether having a very high proportion of persons with academic qualifications makes sense both for the labour market as well as for students who become burdened with debt, in particular due to the high student fees which are almost impossible to repay. It is taking longer to find a job post-qualification, and there are increasingly fewer opportunities of finding employment which appropriately reflects the level of training (WOLF et al. 2016). Many academic graduates are found to be working in inappropriate jobs, and the earnings for many with an academic qualification are barely higher than those for non-graduates. The specialism studied and the educational institution attended are both determining factors in this regard. There are estimates showing that 80 per cent of students in the United Kingdom will never be able to pay off their debts.

Government financing is a key control mechanism. Currently, universities are only incentivised financially to offer *degree* programmes of a maximum length and with a maximum level of fees. The consequence of this is that one- and two-year vocational programmes are developing into three-year bachelor's courses of study (WOLF et al. 2016). This is likely to draw

---

3   These figures relate to the United Kingdom because no data is known to exist for England only.

4   One factor is the upgrading of qualifications in English nursing training from a diploma at Level 5 of the EQF to a full higher education qualification, a process which was essentially completed in 2013. However, even if this development is not taken into account, the decrease in HNCs, HNDs and FDs in the United Kingdom is still almost 45%.

provision towards these programmes and therefore encourage further growth in the numbers of graduates. The supposition is that students who would otherwise have actually selected a short course of study or a practical or pre-vocational course of study are forced to opt for a bachelor's programme (*full degree*) due to a lack of alternatives.[5] It is also suggested that this effect is being accelerated by current efforts to develop existing institutions into universities (WOLF et al. 2016). This could result in more aggressive marketing which has already been observed in other systems, for example in Australia. The only chance for two-year practical and vocationally-oriented training courses is if the funding system changes. The current tertiary education system in England is described by Wolf et al. as being "dysfunctional" (WOLF et al. 2016) – at least when viewed from an overall economic perspective.

On the other hand, PARKER (2017) draws the conclusion from his analysis that *apprenticeships*[6] in the tertiary education sector might fill the void between technical capabilities, employment and higher-level education and training.

Filling this void has been on the educational policymaking agenda in England for many years. The introduction of the two-year FDs in 2001/2002 with the guarantee of progression on to a bachelor's programme in the form of a top-up year marked the start of a far-reaching change in the vocational tertiary sector. Combined with reforms to HNCs and HNDs, the established higher-level vocational qualifications, this resulted in an overall weakening of this very qualification from the perspective of some observers (WOLF/DOMINGUEZ-RAIG et al. 2016). FDs were introduced due to the growing concerns that a shortage of necessary skilled workers might be created in the intermediate qualification area (as presented in the DEARING REPORT (1997)). It was felt that the existing HNC and HND qualifications had lost the essential link to the employers and were therefore no longer supported by them (DEPARTMENT FOR EDUCATION AND SKILLS 2000, GALLACHER et al. 2009). In 2011/12, FDs had largely displaced HNCs and HNDs in the higher education sector, and new registrations reached an annual peak of 80,000. This figure had fallen by half by 2015/16, whilst the number of students in HNC and HND programmes also reduced further.

The *higher apprenticeships* for Level 5 and above of the EQF were introduced in 2008. These can lead on to a university qualification (FD or higher) or to qualifications within the vocational education and training sector which come under *Further Education (FE)* in England.

The *degree apprenticeships* followed in 2015. These are restricted to the higher education sector and are supported by the public purse in the shape of payment of one third of the student fees (see HIPPACH-SCHNEIDER et al. 2016, pp. 13ff.).

Degree apprenticeships

According to EN_M_2,[7] there is huge enthusiasm in policymaking in England for *higher* and *degree* apprenticeships. At the time the interviews were conducted, however, the numbers of participants were relatively low. The training courses for the *degree apprenticeships* in particular are more expensive than *apprenticeships* at the lower level of training, whilst at the same time the government budget is very restricted. EN_M_2 assumes that *degree apprenticeships*

---

5 One further issue regardless of the longer course duration for fully fledged bachelor's programmes is that academic requirements may lead to a reduction in practical content.

6 The definition of *apprenticeship* in the United Kingdom: A paid job with training that leads to a qualification with a minimum duration of 12 months, at least 30 hours a week and 280 hours of guided learning in the first year. This is regulated in a contract with an employer (CIPD 2016).

7 Interviews were conducted from policymaking research level at the end of 2015 with a university representative who had an appropriate research specialism (EN_R), with a government representative (EN_M_2) and with a representative of a sector-based organisation (EN_M_1).

are much more straightforward to implement because universities are able to develop a programme within a short space of time and offer the higher education element of such a programme on the basis of their authority to award degrees. They do not face the constraints of the vocational education and training system and its *awarding bodies*[8] and are not subject to external regulations (EN_M_2).

EN_R fears that *degree apprenticeships* may result in a cutting off of advancement opportunities for learners who start their apprenticeship at a lower level. Employers might tend to recruit apprentices with A Levels[9] to these higher programmes (EN_R). At the very least, a preference is indicated among the major employers in the two English case studies for the recruitment of A-level students for the *higher/degree apprenticeships*. This concords with a report from 2016 (LESTER 2016), which identified a high degree of competition for training places in the most prestigious programmes whilst also simultaneously revealing a tendency on the part of employers to recruit their apprentices from the same applicant pool as the universities. On the other hand, there are several work-based degree programmes which are explicitly aligned towards people in assistant-level and paraprofessional roles to progress to professionally qualified level (e.g. from teaching assistant to teacher). Some of these courses of study could also be offered as *degree apprenticeships* (see ibid.).

Both EN_M_2 and EN_M_1 note that in England many graduates of STEM subjects do not then gain employment in the relevant area. However, according to EN_M_1, graduates of *higher or degree apprenticeships* in the area of engineering remain loyal to the sector. This matches the experiences of the employer in case study 1, who confirmed that *degree apprentices* had a much greater loyalty to the company than the regular university graduates.

EN_M_1 sees no major difference between the *degree apprenticeships* and the so-called "sponsored students" whose part-time degree is financed by the employer. For example, sponsored students and degree apprentices studied together in both of the programmes investigated in the case studies. However, a difference was evident in how both groups were treated within the company. In the case of the employer for English case study 1, a major company, *degree apprentices* were really also viewed as learners, receiving specific support and preparation for the areas where they would later be deployed. At the time of the interview, this was not the case for sponsored students with the same employer, although this was due to change in the future (see 3.3.1).

Developments over recent years in the tertiary sector

For many years, the extremely complex system of vocational education and training has been subject to constant politically driven change. According to statements by all three interview partners, at the time of the interviews at the end of 2015 it was in the midst of the most comprehensive restructuring undertaken thus far. "We have never had until now such a massive change in education and training within this country" (EN_M_1, 01:01:10). At the same time, a pronounced "academic drift" was also occurring in England which, in the view of interview partner EN_R, was partly due to academic requirements, but was also very much driven by "the push for expansion of higher education" (EN_R, 08:05).

A number of sectors in England traditionally had *apprenticeships* which extended over a period of several years and provided a clearly stipulated *progression route* from the current

---

8   Awarding bodies are institutions which are entitled to issue degrees. There is a large number of such institutions in England.

9   A Levels lead directly to a higher education entrance qualification and are comparable to the upper secondary school leaving certificate in Germany (Abitur).

training programmes at EQF Level 3 and 4 on to Level 5 EQF and beyond.[10] The duration of an *apprenticeship* was generally four years, and the purpose was also to develop a vocational identity and expertise (EN_R). This model was broken up by government interventions, and the training was fragmented into smaller sections with no guarantee of progression (EN_R). EN_R regards the lack of guaranteed progression for *apprenticeships* as the major weakness in the system and as indicative of the quality issues. Although this particularly affects areas below the tertiary sector, it is also relevant with regard to a lack of progression opportunities between vocational education and training at the lower levels of the EQF and *degree apprenticeships*.

As described above, HNCs and HNDs were partially superseded by the introduction of FDs (EN_R). In the years following 2001, FDs received strong support and became "flavour of the month" (EN_M_1). They made it possible for universities to access academically weaker applicants as a new target group for the undergraduate sector (EN_R).[11] English case study 2 shows that universities went on the offensive among employers in the region in promoting a switch from HNDs to FDs, which were being newly offered at the time (see 3.3.1).

HNCs and HNDs, which are actually the traditional progression routes in the vocational education and training sector, are also offered by universities. The *awarding body* which holds the rights to these training courses allows universities to develop their own versions under a franchise system. These may differ from one another in terms of content and may also not correspond to the vocational version listed in the qualifications framework, which is a mandatory element of some *apprenticeships* at a higher level. This can lead to problems with recognition of training or where there is a change of training provider (EN_M_1). In the view of interview partner EN_M_1, many universities are now offering FDs as their own version of HNDs.

After the initial financial support was withdrawn, many universities removed the FDs from their range of courses or licensed *further education colleges* (FE colleges) to run these courses (EN_R). For example, the university in case study 2 now only offers the foundation degree investigated. All other foundation degrees in the faculty have been outsourced to an *FE college* (see 3.3.1). This feature of the English system is referred to as *higher education in further education*. Some FE colleges are also entitled to award degrees themselves and offer their own foundation degrees. In this case, however, progression options must be negotiated with universities separately, and there is no guarantee of a bachelor's "top-up" or of full crediting of prior learning for entry to a bachelor's programme.[12]

The weakness caused by uncertainties in the scope for progression and in the lower value attached to vocational qualifications encourages the expansion of academic programmes, as described above. According to EN_R, learners who earlier would have opted for the full-time vocational route are now aiming for a bachelor's degree.

Reform of the apprenticeship and vocational education and training system

Even prior to the introduction of *degree apprenticeships*, the existing *apprenticeship system* had been reformed in the preceding years with the aim of making it generally more attractive and of expanding the system. This issue was a major focus of the interviews conducted at the end

---

10 High-ability apprentices were frequently known to obtain an HNC or HND alongside their work and sometimes went on to achieve full professional status and membership of an association as, for example, a "chartered engineer" or "certified accountant" (at bachelor's or master's level).

11 The undergraduate sector in England encompasses foundation and bachelor's programmes as well as qualifications which are in lesser use today, such as the Certificate and Diploma of Higher Education.

12 The negotiations between the employer in case study 1 and the university provide an example in this regard. The employer would like it to be the case that higher apprentices can enter the second year of the bachelor's degree with their foundation degree qualification from an *FE college* (see 3.3.1).

of 2015. The government had also set the target for three million people to have started an *apprenticeship* within five years by 2020 (DEPARTMENT FOR BUSINESS INNOVATION AND SKILLS 2015). The statistics show, however, that the number of new training contracts fell by five per cent to 495,000 between 2011/12 and 2016/17. Currently (as of December 2017), 912,000 persons are in training. Although the proportion of *advanced* (EQF Level 4) and *higher* (EQF Level 5+) *apprenticeships* has risen over the course of time, these still account for only just under half of all training contracts. In the case of the *higher apprenticeships*, the proportion in 2016/17 was only seven per cent (POWELL 2018).

The reform is interesting when considering the tertiary education and training sector, as *higher apprenticeships* with vocational (partial) qualifications are also affected. The reform of the *apprenticeship system* is part of a reform of the overall FE sector. This was being implemented at the time of the interviews. However, the experts interviewed heavily criticised the government approach. Under an implementation plan for the reform adopted in 2013, initial *trailblazer standards* were to be developed for new training occupations under the overall leadership of groups of at least five employers. The intention is that these standards will gradually replace the *apprenticeship frameworks* which themselves have only been in place since September 2011 (EN_M_1). Unlike the *degree apprenticeships*, these standards will no longer be required to include qualifications (such as HNCs or HNDs). They will, however, need to include an *end assessment*. So far no clarification has been provided regarding the form this will take. These assessments will be offered by an accredited *Apprentice Assessment Organisation* and are planned to lead to recognition by a professional organisation where relevant. The intention is thus that the training itself will become the qualification. Nevertheless, the concern has been expressed that the absence of a permanent qualification could affect the occupational opportunities of those completing the programme in the long term (PULLEN and CLIFTON 2016). The standards themselves comprise just two pages and contain no curricula. "Content isn't part of the process" (EN_M_2, 11:58). Very few guidelines exist relating to these standards. One of these is an obligatory proportion of at least 20% for learning outside of work.

Interview partner EN_M_2 believes that those responsible in the government department regard the implementation of *apprenticeships* as something for which the training provider is responsible and not the employer. The reform therefore raises high expectations among employers without preparing them sufficiently for the development of the standards and without consulting them in the process (EN_R, EN_M_2). In his view, employers essentially use the standards to make requests to training institutions without themselves having to take responsibility. As a result of the constant reforms, institutions in the FE sector are, however, now quite risk averse. They therefore prefer to bide their time regarding innovations if it is unclear whether a market exists (EN_M_2). This has already led to frustration among employers because the training according to their new standards is not yet under way (EN_M_2).

EN_R questions the quality assurance and *governance* of the reformed system. This interview partner explains that no reviews are carried out regarding whether the employer is in a position to carry out the *training* and the *assessment* (EN_R). Learning at work appears to play barely any part in the development (EN_M_2) although according to guidelines this may comprise up to 80%. EN_R explains that quality assurance of the work-based element of the training was very unclear at the time of the interview. EN_R assumes that implementation will involve a broad range of practices both good as well as bad.

The new standards can be developed by a group of employers without the backing of the entire sector. This might reduce their transferability and therefore diminish the value for the individual (EN_R). EN_M_2 criticises quality assurance in the approval of the new standards. "...quality control in terms of getting standards agreed isn't really, isn't really there. The em-

phasis is on getting as many standards as possible so we can reach the three million target"
(EN_M_2, 00:38:16.3).

Part of the reform also involved the introduction of a training levy for companies (*apprenticeship levy*) and the creation of a quality assurance authority, the *Institute for Apprenticeships* (IfA) in April 2017. The IfA is responsible for quality assurance of the training standards and end assessment but not for the actual implementation of training. At present (as of December 2017), the IfA is allocating occupations to broader occupational fields in order to be able to align *apprenticeships* and the new *T Levels* (see below).

At the same time as the reorganisation of the *apprenticeship system*, further reforms relating to the tertiary education and training sector were also taking place in England at the time of the interviews. For example, there was a call for tenders for the creation of *national colleges*, the purpose of which is to offer high-quality education and training programmes in key industrial sectors. None of the consortia involved in the existing FE colleges was successful in the process with the result that entirely new institutions are being created at a time when resources are in short supply (EN_M_2). For EN_M_2, this shows how little the government values what already exists. As part of so-called *area reviews*, existing FE colleges are being inspected with the goal of significantly reducing the number of providers in the respective areas. The remaining institutions will be able to become *institutes of technology* (EN_M_2).

One reform taking place below the tertiary sector is the development of a new group of vocational courses at Level 4 of the EQF designated as *T Levels* (*Technical Levels*). The aim in future is for these to provide a third main progression route for 16-year-olds alongside *A levels* and *apprenticeships*. The intention is for them to be based on standards drawn up by employers in the same way as the *apprenticeships* and to form a bridge between school and employment or continuing vocational education and training. *T Levels* are being developed in 15 broad occupational fields. Their scope will be similar to that of three *A levels*, and they will also include a practical placement. The plan is to expand the remit of the IfA to encompass supervision of this new training pathway.

EN_M_2 views the reforms in vocational education and training as a major challenge. "So you're trying to increase quality, raise the skill levels and expand the numbers with a decreasing budget" (EN_M_2, 06:22). In the view of EN_R, the implementation of the *apprenticeship system* reform was "… very rapid to meet political goals, with little standing back and asking what we really want to achieve" (Part II, 00:02:56). EN_M_1 also criticises the government's approach: "The trouble is they bring in a policy and a lot of the policies at the minute, a lot of the stuff we have been working on for years and years is going to be thrown away" (08:40).

Conclusion

Universities and vocational education and training institutions in England have very different requirements – both with regard to public funding as well as in the development of their provision. While it is generally straightforward for universities to develop and offer new courses of study such as the *degree apprenticeships*, the system of vocational education and training is extremely complex and for many years has been in a process of constant change heavily driven by policymakers.

For the introduction of *apprenticeships* in the tertiary sector, this means that it is probably significantly easier to implement *apprenticeships* which include a university degree. These also receive a huge amount of support, and the government is therefore making them an attractive alternative to the regular and sponsored courses of study for both students and employers. Current figures (UNIVERSITIES UK 2017) show high proportions for *engineering* (20%) and for *digital technology* (33%). General *management training* courses of study account for a proportion of 36%. Nevertheless, the number of *degree apprentices* – for whom the estimate of new training contracts over the three years to 2017/18 is 7,611 – make up under one per cent of total apprentices and all students at Levels 6 and 7 of the EQF, a very low proportion.

Apprenticeships leading to a higher education qualification have thus far tended to result in an independent elite model with no link to training programmes at the lower levels which does not offer any possibility of connectivity for those completing other vocational education and training programmes. This could further weaken vocationally-oriented higher education programmes at Level 5 of the EQF and the vocational education and training system as a whole. On the other hand, new routes for advancement could also open up for persons with assistant qualifications. In addition, employers may see greater opportunities arising from active participation in the training of skilled workers for their company, and this might impact positively on their involvement in training at all levels.

Descriptions by the interview partners imply that there is a strong degree of reform for the sake of reform in the implementation of the *apprenticeship system*, this being primarily focused on achieving the ambitious political goal of three million training positions by 2020. The government opted for the approach of only involving employers in the reform and is therefore excluding key stakeholders such as professional associations, training institutions and unions. This has hindered developments in some areas, particularly in the case of *apprenticeships*, which need to lead to qualified status from a professional organisation or to some form of official registration if they are to be truly accepted. In practice, the employer groups have tended to involve the professional organisations in the development of the standards although they have not necessarily included the other traditional stakeholders in the process.

The interview partners doubt the sustainability of the measures and have clearly expressed their frustration regarding this. The extent to which reform will impact on *higher apprenticeships* outside the higher education sector remains to be seen.

3.2.2   Ireland

Tertiary education in Ireland takes place in the higher education sector and to a very limited extent within the area of vocational education and training. From a national point of view, vocational education and training is seen as part of the *further education* sector,[13] which is aligned to Levels 1 to 6 of the Irish Qualifications Framework (*National Framework of Qualifications, NFQ*), the equivalent of Levels 1 to 5 of the EQF. There is a traditional dual VET system (*apprenticeship system*), although this only encompasses a small number of occupations and sectors. These occupations are aligned to Level 6 of the NFQ (Level 5 EQF) and are thus considered to be an example of work-based tertiary vocational education and training within the project context. In national terms, they are categorised as being post-secondary.

In the *higher education sector, higher education (HE) sector,* qualifications are offered at Levels 6 to 10 of the NFQ (Levels 5 to 8 EQF). The *Institutes of Technology (IoTs)*, which could be described as the Irish "universities of applied sciences" and have their origins in vocational education and training, are of particular interest to the project.

In recent years, educational and VET policy in Ireland has been strongly influenced by the economic crisis, which badly affected the country after 2008 and led to a rapid rise in unemployment. One of the major objectives of the government was to get people back into work. For this purpose, new training opportunities including elements of work-based learning were also created in the tertiary sector to bring participants into direct contact with companies via prac-

---

13   In Ireland, *further education* includes initial and continuing vocational education and training as well as encompassing provision such as literacy courses and *community education*.

tical phases. The *Springboard* initiative (see below), for example, enabled unemployed persons to complete courses in the higher education sector of a duration of up to one year, which in some cases included a proportion of work-based learning.

Comprehensive reforms took place in Ireland's educational and VET sector, and these also created a realignment of the institutional landscape. A dedicated vocational education and training authority (*SOLAS*) was, for example, founded to assume responsibility in areas such as the traditional dual training occupations. *SOLAS* is an adjunct to the *Higher Education Authority (HEA)*, which is in charge of financing and general policy setting in the Irish state higher education sector. A merger of several institutions also led to the emergence of a single state authority in the shape of *Quality and Qualifications Ireland (QQI)*, which awards qualifications in vocational education and training and in the area of higher education in some cases.[14]

In the meantime, the economic situation has improved again and the need for skilled workers is growing in some economic sectors. The Irish Government published its "National Skills Strategy 2025" at the start of 2016. One focus of the strategy is to pursue further development of the FE sector in order to achieve a "...more balanced portfolio of skills development opportunities across the FET and HE sectors" (DES 2016, p. 76). The aim is that vocational education and training should constitute an independent pathway to *skilled employment* (ibid.) rather than merely being viewed as a possible passage to higher education. At the same time, endeavours are being undertaken to achieve a stronger degree of integration, cooperation and partnership between the two sectors (ibid. p. 58).

The strategy accords a high level of importance to work-based learning, and further objectives include increasing the number of dual training and *traineeship* places[15] to 50,000 by the year 2020. This goal was set out in specific form when the "Action Plan to expand Apprenticeship and Traineeship in Ireland 2016–2020" was published in early 2017. The plan aims "to establish work-based learning as a core contributor to our growth as a society and economy" (DES 2017, p. 3). It reflects previous experiences and creates a framework for the further approach to be adopted until the year 2020.

The decision to expand the dual training system was taken in 2014 with a view to adding new occupations and extending up to higher levels within the NFQ. To this end, calls for proposals for new training occupations were instigated in both 2015 and 2017. These were directed at consortia under the lead management of employees. Based on the proposals received, nine new *apprenticeships* were introduced at Levels 6 to 9 of the NFQ (5 to 8 EQF) by December 2017. 49 further new apprenticeships at Levels 5 to 10 of the NFQ (4 to 7 EQF) are at the development or pre-development stage, see SOLAS (2017).

An *Apprenticeship Council* headed by a company representative was created to support and control the process of expansion of the system. It was composed of other representatives from areas such as trade and industry, the social partners and state institutions in the VET and higher education sectors.

---

14 The state universities and the *Dublin Institute of Technology* are permitted to award their own qualifications. The intention is to present a new draft law which will allow other *institutes of technology* to do the same in future.

15 Traineeships are work-based programmes at Levels 4 and 5 of the Irish Qualifications Framework (NFQ). They are developed and offered by the regional Education and Training Boards (ETBs) in the VET sector in conjunction with employers.

Developments in the higher education sector

Far-reaching reforms have also taken place in Ireland's higher education sector over recent years. The aim was to reduce the number of higher education institutions and afford the IoTs the opportunity to amalgamate and attain the status of a *technological university* (IE_M_1).[16]

From the point of view of the interview partners IE_M_1, Ireland has more than enough people with a bachelor's degree whilst the number of qualifications achieved at Level 6 of the NFQ (Level 5 EQF) is falling. In the years leading up to 2006, the primary higher education funding focus was on research. The assumption was that industrial production would be out-sourced from Ireland. A rethink is now taking place, and efforts are being made to redirect higher education institutions back to a stronger commitment to qualifications at Level 6 of the NFQ. The process of converting some of the IoTs into *technological universities* is playing an important role in terms of securing provision at Level 6 of the NFQ in a targeted way (IE_M_1).

The expansion of cooperation between the institutes of higher education and companies is a crucial component of the so-called strategic dialogue (IE_M_1) between the former and the HEA in which consultations take place regarding the main thrust of collaboration in future.

The "Springboard" initiative

The interview partners IE_M_1 view the "*Springboard*" initiative as a milestone in many ways.

The initiative was launched in 2011 with courses in the higher education sector and was coordinated by the HEA. Courses were put out to tender and paid for via the *National Training Fund*, which is mainly financed via an employer levy. The aim of the courses was to enable job seekers to achieve direct re-entry to the labour market. For this purpose, employers were frequently involved in the development of courses content, and practical company-based phases of learning were also integrated. In the area of information and communications technology (ICT), for example, full-time programmes of one year's duration were offered. These consisted of a nine-month course at an institute of higher education and a three-month practical placement and made up around a third of a regular higher education qualification. Many modules included in the courses were part of the normal provision offered by institutes of higher education. There were, however, also specific additional modules. These were used by industry to integrate their own concrete requirements into the courses. "Springboard is the vehicle for them to get that stuff on curriculum" (00:26, IE_M_1_B).

At the time when the interviews were held, around three quarters of those who had completed the Springboard programme were no longer looking for work. For interview partner IE_M_1_A, this illustrates the importance of direct cooperation with employers and of practical work-based elements. This is not yet the rule. "...we don't have a very strong tradition for example of industry and academia working together. This is something quite new we are encouraging" (21:00, IE_M_1_B).

Within the scope of *Springboard,* private institutes of higher education were funded via the *HEA* for the first time. The HEA is normally only responsible for the financing of state institutes. The initiative has also led to the creation of a new model which can be expanded in quantitative terms and is also capable of transfer to other contexts. In the opinion of the interview partners IE_M_1, this is also an important recognition on the part of the ministry. Close cooperation between various ministries is a further new element which has been brought about by Springboard. The initiative may also be helping to increase the likelihood in future

---

16 Interviews were conducted with representatives of two state institutions. Interview IE_M_1 was a group interview with three persons.

that employers will be prepared to share in the costs of education and training programmes. The interview partners also thought it probable that the positive experiences of Springboard and the new cooperation arrangements had helped inform planning of the new training occupations (IE_M_1).

New apprenticeships

With regard to the new training occupations, all interview partners adopt the same view as that expressed in England in expecting that institutes of higher education could be able to offer new training occupations within a short space of time by using their own validation processes. The vision which interview partner IE_M_1_A has for the new system is the creation of a continuum which will allow entry to take place at Level 6 of the NFQ (Level 5 EQF) and enable training to be continued at the higher levels.

There was previously very little networking within the ministry between the areas responsible for vocational education and training and higher education (IE_M_1). However, the whole process of introducing new training occupations has brought huge changes in its wake at a policy level. "…there has been a huge policy reshuffle as well…" (34:33, IE_M_1_C). The *Apprenticeship Council* was founded, and this led to the assumption of a stronger supervisory role by the ministry, a function actually exercised by SOLAS in the traditional training sector (IE_M_1). The calls for proposals for the new training occupations was jointly organised by SOLAS, QQI and HEA. This proved to be a hard process because of the different interests involved (IE_M_1).

Interview partner IE_M_2 is a member of the Apprenticeship Council and reports of protracted and difficult discussions on the distribution of roles of the institutions involved within the process hitherto. "We've spent a huge amount of time over the last number of months in just trying to work through the roles of the agencies in terms of this" (00:21:31). The proposals submitted by the consortia illustrate different scenarios for possible role distributions in the new training occupations. Some of the consortia were initiated by employers directly, whereas in other cases educational establishments were the driving force. A further challenge is provided by detailed questions relating to the nature of the involvement of the higher education sector in the new training occupations (IE_M_2).

IE_M_2 sees the new training occupations as a very interesting diversification of learning at higher levels which in turn opens up enormous opportunities for the educational system. IE_M_2 does not, however, believe that the full extent of these possibilities has been grasped at a policy level. "So I don't think at a conceptual level the opportunities that this presented and the, the change this represented potentially for the education and training system was fully understood (27:49)". For this reason, political support was, for example, lower than that shown in the case of the adoption of the Higher Education Strategy.

The high number of submissions made in response to the call for proposals came as something of a surprise. Different views also came to light in the *Apprenticeship Council*. Some members still tend to see the new training occupations as a possible resort for learners who would actually have preferred to enter the traditional higher education sector. Notwithstanding this, "…as opposed to being your last option, it might be your option of choice" (00:27, IE_M_2). IE_M_2, however, also perceives a change and development in the relevant evaluations in this regard. Nevertheless, essential details are only now being clarified in a process running in parallel to the development of the new training occupations. At the time of the interview, according to IE_M_2, the consortia are driving forward development whilst the *Council* attempts to keep pace.

One key question, for example, is what it means to establish nationally valid standards for the new training occupations if these standards are drawn up by different consortia. Securing the sustainability of the qualifications and deciding on how to deal with changes in the new occupational fields are issues which still need to be clarified. Aspects such as the degree of centralisation of areas of responsibility, financing, designation and awarding of the qualifications and contract design all still continue to form objects of detailed debate in the *Apprenticeship Council*. As far as the future is concerned, IE_M_2 is hoping for the provision of sufficient resources for the process and for appropriate marketing of the new training occupations.

In the categorisation used in the traditional training system, all occupations were aligned to the NFQ as a group at Level 6 (Level 5 EQF) with a view to being subjected to validation by QQI later. Within this context, QQI developed *professional award-type descriptors* at Levels 6 to 10 of the NFQ (Levels 5 to 8 EQF). These descriptors will facilitate future alignment to the NFQ of higher vocational education and training qualifications which are yet to be created. In specific terms, these new descriptors could be used for alignment at higher levels of the new training occupations which are not categorised as belonging to the higher education sector (IE_M_2). All interview partners believe that these descriptors will play an important part in the recognition of prior learning.

Conclusion

In introducing the new training occupations in the tertiary education sector, the government is creating alternative training pathways in order to get people into work and provide trade and industry with the required skilled workers. One essential component of the process is the integration of practical experience with a view to improving the usability of the qualification on the labour market. A further aim here is for companies to be more closely involved in contributing to the cost of training. In the case of training programmes already developed or at the development stage, there is a clear dominance of provision at the higher levels of the NQF. This shows a particular requirement in this area of the educational system, leading to the assumption that these models which involve higher education institutions are likely to be most comparable with the model of dual courses of higher education offered in Germany.

Because the institutional landscape in the area of vocational education and training was redesigned only a few years before the interviews, the beginning of the development of the new *apprenticeships* and the conducting of the interviews at the end of 2015 occurred during a time when newly created and existing institutions were having to define their positioning vis-à-via one another and establish new cooperation arrangements. Although this resulted in friction, it has also facilitated the development of a sense of partnership amongst the individual institutions.

The Irish Government is seeking to integrate the main stakeholders and is thus pursuing an approach aligned towards consensus as the system is developed further. At the same time, trade and industry are also being accorded a key role in this process. The aim of the approach is to establish nationally valid qualifications and sustainable structures in the educational system.

3.2.3   Austria

Debates on necessary changes to the university system have also been ongoing in Austria since the 1980s. The consequences of educational expansion and the expectations invested in this process have been the main cause of and trigger for this discussion (Ö_M_1r[17]). Consideration

---

17   Group interview with partners from the field of research (r) and a trade and industry-related organisation (t).

was given in the past to ideas such as turning the higher vocational education schools (BHS) into universities of applied sciences, although this did not take place for a variety of reasons. In particular, no agreement could be reached regarding the status of the existing BHS teachers.

At a relatively late stage universities of applied sciences were subsequently introduced in Austria on the basis of a law promulgated in 1993. For some time, there have been calls from within this sector for universities of applied sciences to be accorded the right to award doctorates, although the relevant ministry tends to take a critical view of this aspiration (Ö_M_3[18]). The wish is for the universities of applied sciences to maintain a clear alignment to practical academic courses of study and for any loosening of this profile to be avoided. "Labour market data" is crucial to state funding. Targeted state financing of dual courses of higher education is not viewed as being necessary since universities of applied sciences are able to cover the requirement for practice-related programmes by dint of their close association with trade and industry (Ö_M_3). Although this interview partner states that the dual study model is ideal in principle for universities of applied sciences, Austria has a lack of major companies. The commitment in terms of content and financing which such firms are able to provide is considered to be an important factor in the establishment of dual courses of higher education study. However, over the past few years, four dual study programmes have been developed in the area of electrical engineering. In overall terms, about half of programmes at universities of applied sciences are offered on an in-service basis, i.e. studying while in employment,and are viewed as constituting very good continuing training provision (Ö_M_3).

One of the aims in introducing the universities of applied sciences was to foster permeability between educational sub-systems by making such institutions open to persons with vocational qualifications who had not achieved the upper secondary school leaving certificate. This also created an opportunity to offer in-service study and target group-specific programmes of shortened duration. Although this objective is formulated accordingly in the Universities of Applied Sciences Act, very little use of these possibilities has been made.

"All these options to open things up are available in formal terms, but they are only deployed in marginal areas for a range of reasons. One of these is the fact that the university of applied sciences system was subject to close governance by the university system in its start-up phase" (Ö_M_1r). The majority of the members of the University of Applied Sciences Council, which is responsible for accreditation, were persons with university lecturer status. In overall terms, the universities called the academic standard of the universities of applied sciences into question, whereupon they brought about an "academic drift". The joint quality assurance mechanisms which are also in place at the universities have restricted leeway still further.

"All they did was create mini universities. And that is one of the reasons why universities of applied sciences have never emerged in a major way as openly accessible institutes of higher education. Inclusion within this general quality assurance system together with the universities has, so to speak, tightened the reins still further" (Ö_M_1r).

To this extent, the universities of applied sciences have not developed into a provider which offers a wide range of education and training programmes. "…I believe that of 46,000 students at universities of applied sciences, only two or three per cent, at any rate under three per cent, come from the dual system"[19] (Ö_M_1r).

On the other hand, the universities of applied sciences perceive themselves to be "better" providers of vocationally-oriented programmes than the universities because they have the "ear" of trade and industry.

---

18 Interview partner from the Austrian Federal Ministry of Education, Science and Research (BMWF).
19 "Dual system": VET programme in secondary education.

The limited admission capacity of universities of applied sciences means that acceptance of students is decided via entrance and selection procedures. The situation with regard to university courses of study is completely different in many cases. "The universities have to take anyone with an upper secondary school leaving certificate. That is no longer entirely true, because there are now also entrance procedures in oversubscribed courses of study, but this only applies to a small number of programmes" (Ö_M_1t).

According to the opinion of one interview partner, opportunities and areas of potential for the development of innovations in Austria are not necessarily seen as lying in a closer link between companies and institutes of higher education. The expectation is that relevant impetus will emerge from the institutes of higher education. The potential for innovation which can be enlarged and strengthened via cooperation with companies remains largely unrecognised. "… it is certainly the case in Austria that policymakers retain an extremely high degree of trust in tertiary institutions, and this is also the public perception. I think that this is also a basis that makes it very difficult somehow to implement other programmes of study where cooperation between colleagues in these two spheres tends to be intertwined, where persons have occupational experience and where companies also bring their own research and development activities fully to bear in the partnership between the tertiary institutions" (Ö_M_1, 119r).

"Universities in Austria have successfully taken ownership of the role of where knowledge arises within a society. Logically, this function is always exercised by the universities. People need to start by learning this before moving on. What we have not succeeded in making clear [is] that there are various sources of new knowledge" (Ö_M_1, 115r).

Non-formal advanced vocational training

Because around 60% of each age cohort in Austria does not acquire an upper secondary school leaving certificate and the proportion of persons at universities of applied sciences not in possession of such a qualification is only 2%,[20] the interview partner is of the opinion that there is a need for a strong vocational tertiary education and training area which offers programmes which enjoy the relevant degree of recognition and respect (Ö_M_1, 134): "…my hypothesis is firmly held and is that the majority of the public must come from higher vocational education and training that still needs to be defined and lies outside the universities of applied sciences."

At the policymaking level, however, there is currently no need perceived to take action with a view to enhancing the visibility of or improving the reputation of higher vocational education and training in Austria, which is classified as non-formal education. Notwithstanding this, particular endeavours are being undertaken by the Association of Austrian Chambers of Commerce and Industry (WKÖ) to raise the esteem in which advanced and continuing vocational education and training is held as compared to higher education. The intention is also that a professional career should be available via extra-higher education programmes in order to take account of the rising requirements of the labour market in future. Alongside improving permeability between vocational and academic education, there is a particular emphasis currently on strengthening the vocational education and training pathway (Ö_M_1r).

Against this background, the concept of the "University of Cooperative Education" was established in 2014 as a result of an initiative of the WKÖ. "University of Cooperative Education" is an umbrella term for in-service continuing training provision delivered by the organisations involved and should not be understood as being a physical institution. The target group comprises persons in employment at the intermediate qualification level who have completed vocational education and training and gained several years of occupational experience. The joint

---

20 http://statcube.at/statistik.at/ext/statcube/jsf/tableView/tableView.xhtml, last accessed: 15/09/2017

organisation and design concept of the University of Cooperative Education by the WKÖ, WIFI (continuing training academy of the WKÖ), the Vienna University of Applied Sciences and the Vienna Chamber of Commerce and Industry (WKW) ensures that practice-related in-service training can take place at higher education level.

Two-semester courses leading on to (two-semester) master's programmes are offered. The first courses began in September 2014. Programmes currently exist in the two specialisms of commerce and marketing and sales. Students are in their mid to late thirties and have either completed an apprenticeship or attended an intermediate or higher vocational school (usually in the commercial sector). Almost all participants work on a full-time basis, and around 10 to 15% are self-employed.

In order to secure the attractiveness of initial vocational education and training, it was "therefore […] important to us to offer this permeability in accordance with the slogan 'apprentice to master' in the real sense of providing a career pathway" (Ö_M_1t).

The Chamber of Commerce and Industry has already been taking action for a number of years to make advanced vocational education and training more competitive and more attractive. About ten years ago, efforts began in conjunction with German universities of applied sciences and universities in some cases to develop two-year continuing training programmes leading to an academic continuing training qualification and the title of "Master of Science". This title is, however, not recognised as an official "Bologna qualification" and is aligned to the bachelor level with regard to degree of educational attainment.

An initial evaluation of the University of Cooperative Education was conducted in 2015. This revealed a considerable degree of satisfaction on the part of participants with regard to their further occupational development following the continuing training (GRUBER et al. 2015). Study programmes take place on an in-service basis, and companies become involved by funding participation in some cases. There are, however, also cases where companies are not aware of participation in the programmes by their staff. In some instances, the goal of the participants is to prepare for self-employment. In contrast to the so-called basic (*grundständigen*) bachelor's courses of study, which are always free of charge, these two-year educational programmes attract fees of around €2,500 per semester (Ö_M_1t). Universities of applied sciences and universities also offer fee-paying programmes of this type. Their duration varies between two and four semesters.

The development of the University of Cooperative Education originally pursued two objectives. The first was to introduce a hybrid academic vocational qualification in the form of a *Bachelor Professional*. The second aim was to achieve "consolidation" of non-formal continuing training or adult education under a single umbrella whilst making the area of "tertiary VET" or "higher VET" more visible and lending it a clearly recognisable brand name (Ö_M_1r). Regulations for permeability and credit transfer were developed between these two areas. Because of the official "Bologna bachelor's" qualification, this two-part model as originally intended would have had the advantage of connectivity to higher education master's programmes and would thus have been a considerable building block for permeability between vocational and academic education with the potential of illustrating the equivalence of traditional vocational and general or academic educational pathways. This comprehensive concept was discussed within the scope of a ministerial working group but met with a highly critical reception from representatives on the higher education side. It was ultimately shelved following a change of personnel at the top of the ministry responsible.

Conclusion

Tertiary education in Austria involves a clear separation into two areas. Vocational education and training and higher education remain two parallel worlds. The number of persons with vocational qualifications in the university of applied sciences sector is low, and there are few dual study courses.

Some stakeholders, including the WKÖ in particular, view the establishment of a definitive brand for higher vocational education and training programmes which is comparable to the "Tertiary B" sector in Switzerland as an important strategy for improving the attractiveness of VET in overall terms and as something which could exert a knock-on effect for initial vocational education and training (Ö_M_1f, 152).

The central challenge facing VET in the tertiary sector is the creation and firm establishment of an acceptance of "equivalence".

With regard to the question of "academisation" versus "vocationalisation", the interview partners are able to see both processes. The developments verbalised by these two keywords are not mutually exclusive. The numbers of students at institutes of higher education and universities of applied sciences may be referred to in formal terms as "academisation". A "vocationalisation" may also be observed if we look at the educational content and structural design of the programmes. In addition, there is an institutional "upgrading" in areas such as healthcare or social occupations, the institutions of which have been aligned to the higher education sector. This "upgrading" certainly represents a signal of increasing requirements which are becoming ever more complex, despite the fact that the programmes still constitute vocational education and training. An "academisation" is, however, the primarily visible part of the development. The fear is that this could cause the important pillar of higher vocational education and training to pass into oblivion. There is anxiety that "academisation is being taken too far" (Ö_M_1r, 190) and that this could lead to saturation on the labour market.

3.2.4 France

France has been undergoing expansion in the tertiary sector, which exclusively forms part of higher education, since the 1960s.[21] This has been particularly viewed as a way of stimulating economic growth (VINCENS 1995). The particular sustainable growth drivers are, however, two-year practice- oriented study programmes which lead to the qualifications of *Brevet de Technicien Supérieur* (BTS) and *Diplôme Universitaire de Technologie* (DUT) (GIRET 2011, HIPPACH-SCHNEIDER and SCHNEIDER 2016). Both programmes may be completed in the form of an *apprentissage,* i.e. in a school- and company-based combination. To this extent, it is possible to speak of a tendency towards "vocationalisation" in France.

In the same way as countries such as Finland, Norway, England and Ireland, France is also showing a propensity to merge institutes of higher education with a view to gaining greater strength and visibility in terms of international competition. This is seen as bringing much disquiet to the higher education sector (F_R_1).[22] According to the assessment of the interview partner, it will also have consequences for the education and training programmes. He is expecting changes with regard to a reduction in provision and locations and further believes that the merger will decrease human resources and infrastructure costs.

In addition to this, however, France is experiencing academisation via an *upgrading* of training courses. This is occurring in teacher training in particular, which has been elevated

---

21 Advanced vocational training such as that in Germany is not considered to form part of the educational system.
22 The interview partner is a senior researcher in the educational sector and the head of a research institute.

from a bachelor's to a master's course although longer practical phases are also being stipulated (F_R_2).[23] In overall terms, however, this interview partner evaluates the development as a "vocationalisation" of tertiary education.

The view is that the question of labour market relevance is becoming ever more relevant for education and training programmes. There will be very little acceptance in future if tertiary or even academic educational programmes lead to lower positions on the labour market for those completing them (F_R_1). Providers of practice-oriented tertiary programmes[24] are benefitting from a financial grant for a VET tax fund which represents between 0.25% and 1.5% of the annual human resources costs incurred by a company. This additional support is enabling them to offer better conditions of study compared to general higher education programmes (GIRET 2011, p. 248).

The interview partners from the fields of policymaking and research emphasise the high degree of importance of the brief courses of study for the educational system in France. Following a shortening of the programmes leading to the vocational *Baccalauréat professionnel* (Bac Pro) from four years to three, the main educational policy function of the tertiary programmes BTS and DUT has been to take those completing the Bac Pro and to prepare them for an academic course of study. Without these programmes, such persons would not be sufficiently prepared for an academic programme of study (F_M,[25] F_R_1).

Both programmes are aligned to the same level in the ISCED 2011 Classification and in the national qualifications framework (Level III). The main differences are viewed as being that the DUT takes place at institutes of higher education whereas the BTS is mainly offered at secondary schools and that the latter is more professionally specific and more practice-oriented than the former. Despite alignment to the same qualification level, the DUT is seen as being more demanding (F_M, F_R_1). This is also reflected in the fact that these programmes are mainly chosen by school leavers with a general (*Baccalauréat général* = Bac Gen) or technical (*Baccalauréat technologique* = Bac Tec) higher education entrance qualification. Very high proportions of these persons also go on to complete the one-year *Licence professionelle* (LP) programme, which leads to a vocational bachelor's qualification. By way of contrast, approximately two fifths of those completing BTS programmes subsequently enter the labour market. One thing which is seen as problematic is that there are too few BTS places to meet the rising demand for this transition from secondary to tertiary education (F_M). Evaluation of the BTS programmes is difficult because no data is currently available as to destination two to three years after completion. But the practical orientation of the BTS in particular and transfer to the labour market are seen as the second main function of the programme alongside preparing those who complete the Bac Pro to enter academic study.

The role of the companies in the process of curricular development

Development of a new practice-oriented course in the BTS, DUT and LP programmes fundamentally requires a partnership between employers at regional or local level (GIRET 2011, p. 247). Employers are thus represented in the committees responsible for the development of curricula. Each new education and training course must theoretically be based on a specific demonstrable need.

---

23 The interview partner is a senior researcher in the field of vocational education and training/labour market.

24 This applies to universities, to institutes of higher education and also to secondary schools which offer vocation-oriented programmes.

25 Interview partner from the Ministère de l'Enseignement supérieur, de la Recherche et de l'Innovation.

In the view of one interview partner, who has had extensive experience in the field of educational and labour market research and was a member of a CPC (*Commissions Professionnelles Consultatives*) for many years, one fundamental problem is that such committees contain representatives from employer associations or companies rather than consisting of individual professional experts (F_R_3). In his opinion, this may lead to major discrepancies between real needs and curricula. Indeed, responsibility for specific curricular development rests with national education inspectors, who have close relations with the educational establishments and are frequently felt to represent the interests and perspectives of teachers. In his opinion, the role played in curricular development by professional experts should be reinforced.

Regulations regarding the duration of practical placements are stipulated for the educational programmes at a nationally standardised level rather than being the responsibility of the committees. As far as the *apprentissages* are concerned, on the other hand, the education centres have leeway to structure a change of learning venue in their capacity as providers.

Flexibility or scope afforded to educational establishments in terms of how they implement the programmes varies. The degree of such flexibility is, for example, considerable in respect of the LP programmes as compared to BTS or DUT. This means that greater account can be taken of regional requirements and of the demands of the companies. Nevertheless, this has also created a wide range of programmes which in some cases have even been specifically aligned to the needs of an individual firm (F_R_3). State regulation had accordingly led to a reduction in the number of programmes.

Quality, company organisation

No national standardised regulation is in place in respect of the shape of the *apprentissages* in the tertiary education sector. Such a shape varies between regions, each of which pursues its own policy regardless of the economic situation and benefit for the respective labour market (F_R_3). An ever greater emphasis is being placed on the issue of financing. The regions are seeking to make the companies do more in this regard (F_R_3). Up until now, they have funded the training centres or educational establishments offering *apprentissages*.

F_R_3 stresses that the quality of company-based training is an urgent matter. No real quality assurance is in place for the element of the *apprentissages* which is delivered by the firms. No one has a substantive and systematic overview of the structuring of learning processes in the companies, including the regions. It is not possible for the regions to ensure that training takes place in accordance with all regulations and requirements. This particularly applies in the case of sectors which have had no or very little experience with *apprentissages* thus far. Company-based tutors do not have any formal duties to fulfil and are often left to their own devices by the firms. This interview partner believes that there is a very serious lack of uniform coordination.

Company provision

Social insurance or tax breaks are being offered in an attempt to increase the willingness of companies to provide training places. However, the focus of any decision taken by the firms in this regard is on economic benefits rather than on overall societal responsibility towards young people. In overall terms, the companies view their trainees more as employees than as learners (F_R_3).

The readiness of companies to offer practical placements or more *apprentissage* places varies both between regions and between the different programmes. BTS students experience a very difficult situation in respect of the *apprentissages*. This is a view which emerges from all the interviews. Things are somewhat easier for DUT students, whereas the LP programmes enjoy the best situation in comparative terms. The reasons stated here are that the companies perceive the latter to offer the strongest economic benefit. LP students display the necessary maturity, are motivated and can also be effectively integrated into the work processes in professional terms. As far as the firms are concerned, the LP *apprentissages* constitute a recruitment instrument which also allows for integration into the company (F_EI_CS1_1, _2[26]). The higher the level of the training programme, the stronger the likelihood will be that *apprentissages* will be deployed as a recruitment instrument rather than being perceived as a form of education (F_R_1). For this reason, companies were not interested in students continuing to pursue their studies after completing an *apprentissage.* This is less probable following an LP programme than in the case of a DUT or BTS course. The better knowledge the companies have of the content of educational programmes, the greater the likelihood will be that they are prepared to offer training places or practical placements. This willingness is at its highest when the companies are involved in the development of programmes. The interview partner from an educational establishment is of the opinion that joint curricular development needs to be reinforced.

Apprentissages – an educational policy paradox

Several interviewees highlight the paradox which has emerged between the educational policy objective of introducing and strengthening *apprentissages* and the way in which the programmes are implemented in the companies (F_R_3, F_R_2, F_EI_CS1_1). The *apprentissages* model was originally developed for secondary education with the goal of opening up educational prospects for pupils from weaker social backgrounds who have a particular need for support. *Apprentissages* were approved in the tertiary education sector in 1987, although they have only actually been properly established since 1995. Nevertheless, there are differences in the ways in which *apprentissages* feature in the individual tertiary education programmes. All LP courses are available in the form of an *apprentissage,* but only some DUT and BTS courses offer this model. There are only two examples of *apprentissages* in the area of general bachelor's programmes (F_EI_CS1_1, _2). Advisory centres have also been set up at institutes of higher education with the aim of providing targeted support for *apprentissages* via vehicles such as cooperation agreements with companies (F_EI_CS1_1, _2). A further objective here is to open up more master's programmes of study to *apprentissages*. Within this process, it is proving easier to work with major or larger companies and with certain sectors such as engineering.

32.5% of all *apprentissages* are now conducted in the tertiary education sector (Ministère de l'Éducation nationale de l'Enseignement supérieur et de la Recherche (MENESR) 2016). The companies are also selecting particularly good pupils, something which is no longer in line with the actual intention behind the programmes. Although the introduction of *apprentissages* in the tertiary education sector has had a positive effect on the model of company-based education and training in overall terms, the fact that companies prefer tertiary programmes has placed provision in the secondary sector under additional pressure. At the same time, this means that it is more difficult to demonstrate the benefit of *apprentissages* for transition to the labour market (F_R_2), because this transition is in any case easier for this group of learners and for tertiary sector learners generally. Not to put too fine a point on it, this means that an instrument aimed at disadvantaged young people has become a pathway for high ability students. The company-based education and training system is felt to be very selective (F_R_1).

For this reason, F_R_2 und F_R_3 believe that the coming debates on *apprentissages* will focus on the issue of their benefit for the transition to the labour market and on the question

---

26 Interview with representatives from two companies.

of financing, in particular with regard to the payment of subsidies to companies for making *apprentissage* places available (see also GIRET 2011). Extremely fundamental issues relating to the development of the universities and their role in the educational system with regard to a "vocationalisation" process are, however, also the object of current discussions (F_R_2).

"Work-based learning" as a term

The term "work-based learning" is not truly established and well known in France (F_R_2). The tendency instead is to make reference to "professionalisation", although this is a notion with many meanings. In the experience of this interview partner, opinions on this are contradictory in some cases. Some companies supported a greater degree of vocational orientation in tertiary education programmes, whereas the employer organisations (e.g. MEDEF) were less in favour of this. The Association of University Presidents would also welcome such a development because the universities are in competition with other institutes of higher education in respect of the effects of practice-oriented programmes on transition to and integration into the labour market and these aspects are also reflected in a ranking list. In the view of this interview partner, this represents an attempt to find a short-term solution to the relatively high rate of youth unemployment in France.

Conclusion

Vocational preparation or practice-oriented programmes with the option of an *apprentissage* have been growing in significance in the higher/tertiary education sector in France since the 1970s. Future expansion is in particular linked with the issues of funding, financial and content participation of companies and analysis of the benefits of *apprentissages* for the transition from education to the labour market. These are the major focuses of the debates which are currently ongoing. In France, there is a clear differentiation between secondary and tertiary education with regard to esteem and attractiveness. Practice-oriented education and training in the tertiary sector, in particular in the form of *apprentissages,* is selective and enjoys recognition amongst students as the best pathway for transition to the labour market whereas vocational education and training in the secondary sector is considered to be a second-choice option (GIRET 2011, p. 246).

3.2.5 Norway

The tertiary education sector in Norway is characterised by a binary higher education system which features universities and *university colleges* alongside vocational colleges (*fagskole*).[27] That means that tertiary education comprises higher education and non-higher education. Forms of curricularly interlinked dual courses of study or educational programmes at bachelor level are limited to specific areas such as nursing or training programmes for nursery school teachers at the *university colleges*. Mandatory practical placements are stipulated in some courses of study, although these elements are primarily voluntary. Bachelor's and master's theses in fields such as engineering are, however, increasingly focusing on practice-oriented or company-related topics (NO_M[28]).

In addition, shortened master's courses of study for students with at least two years of relevant occupational experience (so-called *experience-based programmes*) have been in place since 2003. In some cases, those studying in such programmes are required to be working at

---

27 Continuing vocational education and training, e.g. courses leading to the acquisition of a master craftsman qualification, do not form part of the educational system.
28 Interview partner from the Ministry of Education and Research.

the same time and company-related projects are pursued (NO_M). The institutes of higher education are permitted to charge fees for these courses of study, and to this extent they differ from traditional master's programmes.

Higher education policy

In the wake of the *white paper* on "Education Strategy" of 2009, higher education institutions were also required to establish committees with representatives from industry. Some of these committees are working well, others less so (NO_M). The issue of employability plays a major role in higher education policy in overall terms (NO_M).

The main focus in this policy area over recent years has been the merger of university colleges and universities. This has taken place because institutions were perceived as being too small and too fragmented (NO_F[29]).

"And the government is putting quite a big pressure on the institutions" (NO_F, 10).

From the point of view of the ministry, this development formed part of a strategy to improve the quality of higher education. International competition to secure students and researchers was a further aspect (NO_F). Although this merger has led to a reduction in the number of programmes at individual locations in some cases, it has also resulted in enhanced quality. Nevertheless, it will only be possible to analyse the actual effects in a few years' time (NO_M).

On the other hand, there are fears that specialist locations may occur and that this could be to the detriment of the link between the education institutions with a region and its labour market (NO_F). This tendency towards concentration will also affect the *fagskole* over the coming years (NO_F).

The Y-veien – a special programme in higher education for VET-qualified students

Since 2002, Norway has been piloting an innovative approach, particularly in some bachelor's programmes in the field of engineering. The usual educational pathway into the higher education sector is via a relevant general secondary qualification or via a vocational qualification plus completion of a supplementary year. The so-called *Y-veien (Telemark Model)*, on the other hand, permits those who hold a relevant vocational qualification and who also have occupational experience to proceed to the *university colleges* without any requirement to complete the supplementary year. One of the case studies conducted within the scope of the project investigated such a programme (see Chapter. 3.3.5). Although the *Y-veien* bachelor's programme leads to a conventional bachelor's degree, the first-year subjects taken by students with a vocational qualification are varied in accordance with their existing competencies. In some cases, the two groups of students learn in separate courses during the initial semesters, e.g. electronics or mathematics. The aim here is to open up additional permeability for those with vocational qualifications. Several courses of study structured in this way are now in place.

29　Interview partner from a national educational research institute.

Fagskole

A very wide range of programme provision is available in the *fagskole* sector. This includes two-year programmes at EQF Level 5/ISCED 5 for those who have completed upper secondary level or for persons in employment with five years of relevant occupational experience. Shorter programmes from a duration of six months upwards are, however, also on offer. These encompass numerous occupational areas such as construction, the electrical sector, arts and crafts, healthcare and social work and the hotel and restaurant sectors. 60% of participants are in possession of a vocational qualification. About 30% hold a higher education entrance qualification, and around 10% achieve admission via assessment of individual competencies. With the exception of courses in the healthcare sector, these programmes frequently do not stipulate practical placements because participants predominantly have occupational experience and large numbers of programmes are organised on an in-service basis.

In 2014, a government commission was set up to investigate VET in the tertiary sector (NOU 2014). This recommended that the government should strengthen the *fagskole* and turn them into a clear alternative to institutes of higher education. The argument given was that there was a need for qualified skilled workers at this level and that more young people should opt to go in this direction. The Ministry of Education and Research used this recommendation as the basis for drawing up a white paper on the vocational schools (Norwegian Ministry of Education and Research 2016).

This strengthening of the *fagskole* is also supported by the social partners. There is a feeling that the "academisation" of traditional vocational education and training via the launching of appropriate bachelor's courses of study will necessitate the introduction or expansion of shorter educational programmes which are vocationally- and practice-oriented.

The white paper makes a series of proposals for improved visibility and increased attractiveness of the *fagskole*. The *colleges* are encouraged to develop programmes which significantly differ from those offered by the institutes of higher education.

The fundamental goal is to increase the number of students at the *fagskole*, and the intention is to amend the underlying law so that the *fagskole* are officially aligned to the tertiary sector, thus enabling the programmes to be designated in overall terms as "higher vocational education".

There is a desire to increase the influence the employers are able to exert on education and training content and curricula, and to this end each will receive two representatives on the college committees. The plan is to enable the *fagskole* to define occupational experience as an admission requirement and to offer three-year programmes which will put them in direct competition with the three-year bachelor's courses. The rights and status of students will be made equivalent to those of higher education students, and the plan is to award a qualification entitled *Vocational College Candidate* after completion of a one-year programme. The institutes of higher education will become more flexible with regard to admission of those who have completed programmes at *fagskole*, and they will also develop credit transfer mechanisms for the bachelor's programmes.

Vocational Bachelor

A *fagskole* launched an initiative to establish a *Vocational bachelor* qualification in the area of the engineering sciences. Because only the higher education sector is permitted to use such a title, any such programme would need to be "of a higher education nature" (NO_M). However, no need was perceived for an additional bachelor's degree in the area of *engineering* because existing programmes of study in this specialism are already having difficulties in attracting candidates. This formal argumentation was used by the ministry to reject the proposal without taking account of the intended differences between the two "bachelor's" programmes with regard to content design and the different structure of participant groups in terms of prior learning, occupational experience and age (NO_M).

Conclusion

Although the employers are in favour of a more practical alignment of bachelor's programmes, there are currently no plans to pursue a closer link between academic education and vocationally- and practice-oriented education and training by setting up dual courses of study which go beyond those already in place (NO_F). The focus of educational policy is on quality assurance in academic education. The belief here is that this can be improved by amalgamating and merging institutes of higher education (NO_M), although there is also significant criticism of such an approach (NO_F). In overall terms, the interview partner from the Ministry of Education and Research (NO_M) is reticent with regard to giving the companies a greater role in developing educational content for the institutes of higher education because they tend to take a short-term view of skills needs. Nevertheless, the aspect of preparation for the labour market is an important perspective for the shaping and further development of higher education and may have a larger part to play in the next round of reforms (NO_M). Educational committees with employer representation exist at a national level in some sectors (NO_M).

One particular quotation provides a very good summary of the attitude adopted by the interview partner from the ministry:

"...it's – and it's nice to be able to cater for all needs and all types of people because when more and more people go through the education system, you need a variety of offers just to be able to cater for different people" (NO_M, 117).

From the research point of view, the undeniably strong preponderance of the academic sector in tertiary education is not without its problems. "I think, in general, for Norway it should be a concern that sort of that the practice road to the labour market should be developed further, both at the upper secondary level and at the tertiary level. And it's a danger of too large part of the education system, now with the mergers and everything, being forced into the more academic track. So yes, I'm actually concerned about the whole relevance of the education system, both at the upper secondary and at the tertiary level" (NO_F, 79). However, there are some initiatives to strengthen practice orientation and tertiary VET.

Greater inclusion of WBL elements in the training programmes lies within the discretion and area of responsibility of the educational establishments themselves. The general legal conditions certainly permit such a step, and the ministry also has no fundamental objections to relevant initiatives (NO_M). Indeed, policymakers have encouraged this.

3.2.6 Poland

Tertiary education in Poland is higher education. In institutional terms, this includes the universities, the teacher training colleges and, since 2005, the *state schools of higher professional education* (SSHPE). The Law for the Regulation of Higher Education created a legal basis for the integration of the SSHPE into the higher education sector. This means that institutes of higher education all operate in accordance with the same statutory foundations. The SSHPE only differ from the universities in terms of definition of learning outcomes. These are more practice-oriented in the case of the SSHPE. In an international context, they are also often designated as *universities of applied sciences*. Their provision particularly includes bachelor's programmes in the fields of engineering, technology, the economic sciences, education, tourism and foreign languages.[30]

The aim was to use the SSHPE as a vehicle to generate a stimulating effect on the regions and regional economies and supply them with the necessary skilled workers. The law reflects the strongly held policy view that the universities are unable to keep pace with the dynamism of the labour market. The overriding perception was that there was a need for alternative training and educational options (SARYUSZ-WOLSKI et al. 2016). Although these tertiary institutions are significantly smaller than the country's major university centres, they offer the benefit that regional cooperation with companies can be structured in a more direct and straightforward way. They are "nearer to the heart of the action". This cooperation is displayed in a variety of forms. Students are afforded the opportunity to use the laboratories and workshops of the companies within the scope of their studies, and this results in a knowledge of current company technology. At the same time, company-based skilled workers act as lecturers at the universities of applied sciences.

The practical placements included in the programmes are generally voluntary. The universities or state schools are permitted to decide for themselves whether mandatory practical placements should be introduced. Satisfaction with the current arrangements regarding practical placements is limited. Placements are frequently not closely related to the programme of study or else are not of high quality. "…. it doesn't work that well" (PL_F, 44[31]). "So even if there are internships, they are not designed in a way to actually supplement well that the study programmes and, and the curricula at, at, at the university" (PL_F, 44).

Nevertheless, the first so-called dual or in-service programmes of study have been introduced at the SSHPE[32] with the aim of achieving a closer link between higher education and company-based learning and developing pilot programmes. However, the term "work-based learning" or a Polish equivalent has yet to be established (PL_F, 80). The tendency is to speak of practical orientation (PL_F, 54).

Employers largely categorise the university-based bachelor's degree as not providing sufficient vocational and practical preparation. "Namely if you ask employers they don't value people with a bachelor degree very much so basically almost everybody continues education into the master programme" (PL_F, 48).

The idea of strengthening practical and labour market orientation in the higher education sector is somewhat of a new notion. "You should remember that still the most important thing is that our higher education system does not have a lot of this kind of approach towards vocational teaching and practice-oriented courses because this is something that is well a relatively new phenomenon" (PL_F, 111).

Nevertheless, the massive rise in participant numbers at institutes of higher education after 1990 has exacerbated the question of the quality of the programmes. Numerous private institutes of higher education have emerged, and the issue of learning outcomes of higher education programmes in respect of labour market needs and matching has become acute. Although these discussions and considerations regarding a careful reorientation of institutes of higher education have been welcomed, the limitations of such an approach have also been pointed out. University education in particular also represents a foundation for research, and this objective needs to be taken into account accordingly. "And I would still say that the labour market is not the dominant perspective when we discuss what happens in the higher education. That

---

30 There are currently 35 SSHPEs.
31 Interview with two VET researchers.
32 e.g. in Leszno: http://www.pwsz.edu.pl/index.php/en/rekrutacja-4; accessed: 26/09/2017.

it's still like, this is one of the goals but we should not forget that the higher education also service the research development, preparing students for doing research and, and this kind of focus is I think still present quite a lot in the discussions" (PL_F, 111).

The SSHPE are of considerable relevance to the educational system in Poland to the extent that their regional and company proximity and alignment fills a gap in the qualification system. It is, however, not easy for them to hold their own against the university centres. The general reasons for this are the low degree of esteem accorded to vocational education in Poland and a sceptical and hostile attitude from within academic circles (SARYUSZ-WOLSKI et al. 2016). Demographic development is also amplifying the rivalry between education and training providers as they compete to secure students.

Conclusion

The development of the SSHPE in Poland has certainly led to movement within the field of tertiary education, and this has produced a stronger differentiation in the area of higher education in terms of a shift towards vocational preparation and practice-related programmes. Although institutes of higher education have launched initiatives to structure bachelor's or master's programmes of study in a more practice-oriented way, particularly in the engineering sciences, the higher education sector in Poland continues to be highly traditional with regard to the characteristics it displays. In the interviews mentioned, doubts were certainly expressed as to whether high numbers of graduates are useful in terms of employability and labour market matching.

3.3 Interviews with students, companies and educational institutions

The following section evaluates and inter-references the interviews conducted with the students, the companies and the educational institutions. The interviews with the educational institutions always relate to the programmes being studied by the students interviewed. This is not always the case with the interviews conducted with companies, and this circumstance is indicated where relevant.

The main focus is on the interviews with the students. These form the starting point for the analysis and dictate the thematic structure of the presentation. Remarks and statements made by the interview partners from the companies and educational institutions are aligned and correlated accordingly. Supplementary information on thematic areas and aspects not addressed by the students is added subsequently.

The purpose of choosing invented names for the students is to emphasise the qualitative and individual nature of the remarks made. The form of representation used and the personalised style place the perspective of the learners to the fore.

3.3.1   England

Case study 1: "Warwick WMG Applied Engineering Programme (BEng)" at the University of Warwick

Overview of case study interviews

EN_C_CS1_1	Company 1
EN_EI_CS1	Training institution
EN_St_CS1	Students 1 (Tom*) und 2 (Chris*)

*Names altered

Background information[33]

The degree lasts for four years and is offered on a part-time basis. Over the first two years, participants complete six blocks which each last for one week. At the end of the second year, the students decide which specialism they wish to pursue. Each year the students must obtain 90 credits, half of which must be in their specialisation. In terms of content, the degree has the same structure as the relevant full-time degree, but there are some minor differences, for example a higher proportion of specialisation.

Several modules are taught in each block. Examinations are sat as early as after the second block. Lecturers from the university are mainly deployed to teach the basics during the first two years, and from the third year sessions are increasingly run by specialists from industry. Outside of the blocks, participants are supported by a virtual learning environment.

Projects are run with five to six participants from a range of areas as early as the first year of study. The groups keep in contact via the learning platform. Employers are heavily involved in these projects. In the third and fourth year of study, a company-based project is run comprising 15 credits. As part of this, participants are able to structure the project in consultation with the employer so that it meets company requirements. In the process, the university ensures that a project includes the necessary academic element.

At the time of the interview the third cohort was starting the course of study. This is the only bachelor's course of study in the department. All other courses of study culminate in a master's.[34] In 2013 approximately 35 participants started the degree. By 2014 this had already risen to around 70, and in 2015 the figure was 83. Because the majority of participants come from a major employer and have taken a *foundation degree* at a *further education (FE) college* prior to this course of study, the department is already certain it can expect at least 100 participants for the year ahead. Of these, almost 80 will be *higher* or *degree apprentices*. The remainder will be students sponsored by the employer. At the time of the case study there were participants from eight other companies of different sizes.

Of the apprentices from the major employer, all but three have A levels and all come to the university with a Level 3 foundation degree (Level 4 EQF). In future, this employer is planning

---

33 Unless indicated otherwise, all information in this section comes from the interview with the educational establishment. This does not include the footnotes.

34 In the United Kingdom, the duration of courses of study in engineering is generally from four to five years (full-time or part-time equivalent). These programmes then lead directly to a master's qualification (MEng), and this also fulfils the academic requirements for conferment of the status of "Chartered Engineer" by a professional organisation. These requirements may also be met via separate bachelor's and master's qualifications.

to transfer credit from the *FE college* to the programme of study up to Level 4 (Level 5 EQF). This means that students will be able to enter the second year of the study programme directly (Level 5, also Level 5 EQF). At the time of the case study the negotiations relating to this were still under way. The sponsored students generally do not have A levels or have attained them several years previously. The department has therefore developed its own entry test. This takes place in the form of a one-week block before the start of registration. Following this, a few of these sponsored students decide against the course of study. In the first two years, participants are supported by a mathematics lecturer.

It is possible for participants who leave the course early to have a *certificate* or *diploma* issued to them depending on the duration of study. However, this has not yet occurred. Accreditation of the course of study by a professional body is not possible until students have graduated from the course of study. The department is in discussions with a body for this purpose and assumes that accreditation will be granted.

Evaluation focusing on the perspective of the apprentices

At the time of the interview, both participants were in the second year of the study programme and in the fourth year of their *higher apprenticeship* with a large company.

Access

The entry requirement for the *higher apprenticeship* was the A-level qualification. The application for the training programme was followed by an intensive selection process. After completing an online application, applicants worked on mathematics exercises. An assessment centre then followed once this level was passed. Those applicants who also passed the assessment centre were then invited to a final interview. Only one out of every 38 applicants received a training position.

In the first two years of training, the interview partners completed a *foundation degree*. The first year took place on a full-time basis at a *training college* with placements at the company. In the second year, the apprentices spent four days a week in the company and one day in *college*.

Chris grew up with an engineering background in his family, and his career aspirations also took him in this direction. The *higher apprenticeship* was the ideal access point for him. He was aware of the opportunity for company-based training from his father. He did not wish to go straight to university after school and instead selected a more practice-oriented option.

Tom comes from a part of the country which is further away and was proactive in terms of trying to gain a place on this training course. "I've actively run out to this apprenticeship" (00:02:28). For example, he specifically practised interviews.

Course of study

The interview partners can very easily connect what they have learned in the degree with their work in the company: "…when we're learning in a lecture we are always prompted to pop the hand up and say, oh I've seen that at work and I'm going to apply it this way" (Tom, 00:14:17). On the other hand, they think they will not need some of the content in the university modules and then shortly afterwards situations occur in which they can apply precisely this knowledge. This is not always the case of course but there are a lot of "aha" moments.

Both interview partners really value the fact that the majority of lecturers previously worked in industry. Contact with other students also gives them an insight into other areas. Both interview partners also stay in contact with their colleagues during the blocks at the university, and are at least partially contactable.

The second block commences with an examination. Between the blocks, students receive assignments and assessments in preparation for the examinations. They work on these via a learning platform. The learning platform also includes forums and enables lecturers to be contacted directly.

Chris keeps his evenings free during the module, but after this he tries to study each evening during the week. Occasionally slack time occurs at work, which both apprentices are then able to use for studying. Tom also uses his lunch break for studying. Other apprentices have also arranged fixed learning times with their line managers.

Chris and Tom do not yet know what the specialisation options in the degree are after the second year. They assume that their superiors will decide with them which modules they take.

WBL – work and learning

The interview partners are doing their training in the same company but in different areas and in different positions. They are assigned to the area in which they will be working after the training. Assignment to internal company areas took place without detailed information. However, the procedure has now been adapted for subsequent years.

During the training, they are encouraged to complete placements in other areas of the company and are actively supported in this by the training team. "They are saying by the end of the degree we expect you to have gone and seen the business" (Tom, 00:08:00). The idea behind this is that the apprentices will develop an improved understanding of the other areas and that they will apply this knowledge in their job. The focus here is on the personal development of apprentices and on creating networks.

Tom feels like a normal employee in his area. His supervisor looks after him and provides guidance in day-to-day business. In addition to this, there is also a WBL manager who supports apprentices and, for example, ensures compliance with all the necessary learning and safety provisions. He is also the contact in relation to the degree. About once every two months, the WBL manager meets with the apprentices. This meeting is also attended by the department supervisor. Every six months, there is also an apprenticeship review and an annual employee appraisal which relates to the specific job. Besides this there is a training manager who is consulted, for example, when making decisions about business travel.

In overall terms, the *higher apprentices* receive a great deal of support. So far, for example, it has always been possible for them to complete specific training if they wished to. During their time at work, the apprentices also complete NVQs as part of the training.[35] The incentive for them is that every six months they receive a performance-related salary increase.

The apprentices are seen as fully fledged team members in their areas and are treated as fully trained engineers. In Tom's view, however, this does not apply to all *higher apprentices* and instead is largely dependent on management and attitude taken.

---

35 National Vocational Qualifications (NVQs) are competency-based and are based on the National Occupational Standards (NOS). They are examined directly in the workplace or in a simulated work environment. NVQs are now no longer being developed.

View of the company (EN_C_CS1_1)

In addition to the *higher apprentices* (now also referred to as *degree apprentices*), there are also 25 sponsored students on the programme from the large company at the time of the interview. Of these, five have previously completed training in the company. The sponsored students must pass a test as an entry requirement. In contrast to the higher apprentices, there are no mentors for the sponsored students, no ongoing support and no development plan. So far, needed to be a business necessity for the degree but this is to change in future. The company is planning to provide greater support for sponsored students and to better utilise their potential.

The intention is also to plan the recruitment of apprentices more strategically in the future. The company has found that *higher apprentices* offer many benefits compared to regular university graduates. They identify themselves more strongly with the company, are more motivated and willing to learn and above all stay with the employer for a longer period. Other university graduates often come with very high expectations and leave the company after a short period because these expectations are not met quickly enough: "...their expectations are set quite high when they come into this business to say they can achieve this level and move up the ranks quite quickly and that is not always the case" (EN_C_CS1_1, Part II 00:03: 24). For this reason, more *higher apprentices* are already being recruited.

The employer is in regular contact with the university. The individual departments communicate their requirements and the university explains which of these they can implement. A larger project which is agreed with the employer is run in the first year of study.

Satisfaction/outlook

Tom is very satisfied with his training. "I would recommend it to anyone" (00:33:02). He finds the programme very demanding, but also sees the advantages. For example, he is not having to get into debt due to the student fees. "So work is very demanding and to do a degree on top of that is very hard and very stressful but we're all sensible enough to know that we're not getting debt from it, we're not going to struggle to get a job afterwards ..." (00:33:02). A major advantage for him is the six years of professional experience at the end of the programme.

Chris is also very satisfied. "...so four years into it and I don't regret it one bit and I would certainly recommend it to anyone" (00:01:11).

However, both are critical of the *foundation degree*. They are of the opinion that this was not really necessary and was more of a waste of time. At the start in the company there were also a few rules which they did not find very useful for the context in which they were working, for example the ban on travel and overtime for apprentices. However, over time, by actively following this up and with increasing trust, these aspects were managed more flexibly and are no longer an issue. They describe themselves jokingly as "guinea pigs" because they were the first cohort of the higher apprenticeship, but they can also see that their suggestions have been adopted and that the programme is being further developed. For example, the introduction at the start of the training has been significantly extended and a development plan now exists for apprentices.

They feel very happy and the company and are enthusiastic about their work: "...that's what really makes me sort of praise the apprenticeship scheme is because you're treated like normal people. [...] and they make it so that you're empowered to an extent where you are really passionate about your work..." (Tom, 00:44:24). They have been told by the employer that the aim of *higher apprenticeships* is to recruit managers. The employer has a ten-year plan for this purpose. After six years, the apprentices receive the internal status of "C Grade Engineer", and the subsequent aim is that they will take on management responsibility within ten years.

Conclusion

The major company uses the *higher apprenticeship* as a recruitment pathway for future management staff and as an instrument to secure loyalty to the company from those who complete the programme. As would be expected, the company also devotes considerable efforts to looking after its apprentices. The combination of higher education study and company-based training places high demands on the apprentices. At the same time, they very much appreciate the opportunities they have been given and are very performance-oriented.

The case study highlights the problem area of FD qualifications at extra-higher education institutions in respect of which recognition of performance in terms of credit transfer to a bachelor's qualification still needs to be negotiated. It also exemplifies the thesis propounded in Chapter 3.2.1 that recruiting school leavers who have gained A levels to the *higher apprenticeships* makes the internal advancement pathway more difficult for those who have completed *apprenticeships* at lower levels or achieved other vocational qualifications. Secondly, because of the experience it has had with *higher apprentices*, the company plans in future to act internally to provide a similar structure of support for an in-service programme of study to motivated employees who are not in possession of a higher education qualification.

Case study 2: "Electrical and Electronic Engineering Foundation Degree" at the University of Greenwich

Overview of case study interviews

EN_C_CS2_1	Company 1 – SME (small and medium-sized enterprises)
EN_C_CS2_2	Company 2 – state company
EN_EI_CS2	Educational establishment (2 persons)
EN_St_CS2	Students 1 (Liam*) and 2 (Matt*)

*Names altered

Background information[36]

The course of study was established in 2010. At this time there was significant government support for the creation of foundation degree programmes. "Foundation degrees were the flavour of the month" (EN_EI_CS2_2, 00:04:30.7). Due to the mandatory possibility of progressing to a bachelor's degree, *foundation degrees* were regarded as the better alternative to advanced vocational qualifications[37] and, at that time, the staff responsible also endeavoured to convince the regional employers of this. Those responsible identified a gap in the market in this area. Regional employers were involved in the development of the course of study, which also led to the focus on work-based learning.

The course is offered as a part-time course of study and is aimed at employees in the engineering sector. It takes three years to study for a *foundation degree*, and the students attend

---

36 Unless indicated otherwise, all the information in this section comes from the interview with the educational establishment. This does not include the footnotes.

37 Higher National Diplomas (HND) and Higher National Certificates (HNC) are higher-level vocational qualifications at EQF Level 5. These were once the established progression routes for apprentices, but have become less important over recent years. One of the reasons for this has been the introduction of foundation degrees (see also Chapter 3.2.1).

university on one fixed day during the week. Specialisations are available in mechanical engineering and electrical engineering. Just under 20 students are accepted each year. Of these, around seven in each cohort have continued studying with the aim of achieving a bachelor's degree. The bachelor's degree can be achieved over a further two years of part-time study or in one year on a full-time basis. To date, students have only made use of the first option. The percentage transferring should soon increase because one employer with many course participants has announced that all its *higher apprentices*[38] will transfer to the bachelor's programme in future. Progression onto a master's course of study is also possible. The course of study is accredited by the professional body[39] the "Institution of Engineering Technology".

The students generally have around two to three years of occupational experience and are funded almost exclusively by their employers. Many are at the end of an *advanced apprenticeship* (EQF Level 4) and/or have the status of "higher apprentice" (EQF Level 5) in the company. However, there are also "sponsored students".[40] In order to meet admission requirements, some of the students have A levels,[41] some have a vocational qualification (BTEC[42] Level 3, the equivalent of EQF Level 4), obtained via training, and others have both qualifications. At the time of interviewing, this was the first time that the employer who provides many of the students had registered only higher apprentices in its new cohort. These higher apprentices were recruited immediately upon completion of their A levels.

The course of study includes a module on "work-based learning" which can be taken over the entire period of study and comprises one quarter of the overall credits. A further quarter of the credits for the module are obtained from a preparation course, the main focus of which is academic writing. The module also contains a course entitled "Understanding my Organisation" in which students familiarise themselves with their company. For the actual work-based learning, the students have a range of different options comprising 45 credits:[43]

▶ Project work: The students are required to select a topic and define learning goals. They must have this approved by their employer and must agree the details with them. They work on a written report in which they set out the problem and discuss and conduct a professional discussion about the project. This is assessed at the university, but feedback from the employer is also taken into account. Most students choose this option.

▶ Students are, however, also able to acquire some of the credits via vocational training. This training must meet university specifications in terms of level and scope. It is also possible to take additional academic courses. The report is prepared in both cases in relation to the content and in particular the application of what has been learned. A specialist oral examination also takes place. However, only very few students avail themselves of this alternative option.

---

38 Higher apprenticeships in England are at Level 5 to 7 of the EQF https://www.gov.uk/apprenticeships-guide (21.11.2017)

39 Professional bodies play an important role in the practising of many professions in England through the awarding of membership, qualified status or titles such as *"Incorporated"* and *"Chartered Engineer"*. For this purpose, they also accredit education and training courses both within and outside the higher education and vocational education and training systems.

40 Regular employees who have a degree funded by their employer alongside their occupation.

41 Highest level school leaving qualification.

42 BTEC = (former) Business and Technology Education Council, various vocational qualifications equivalent to general education school-based qualifications (GSCE = BTEC Level 2, A level = BTEC Level 3 and "National"). The BTEC qualifications are now awarded by Pearson, a private training company. http://qualifications.pearson.com/en/about-us/qualification-brands/btec.html (09.06.2017).

43 In the United Kingdom, two credits are the equivalent of one credit point in the European Credit Transfer System (ECTS). An ECTS credit is, in turn, equivalent to approximately 25 to 30 hours of work.

There is also a work-based project work worth 30 credits at level 5 (EQF Level 5). The purpose of this is to challenge students and also to serve as a basis for those who are continuing the course of study with the aim of achieving a bachelor's degree.

Evaluation focusing on the perspective of the participants

At the time of the interview, Liam and Matt were in the final year of the *foundation degree*.

Access

Liam works in a medium-sized company with approximately 120 employees, where he is employed as a technician. He started there six years ago as an apprentice in the production area. He has a qualification from a vocational school,[44] a BTEC Level 3 in *electronic engineering*. He subsequently moved from production into the research and design area and began his course of study. He was keen to gain further training and there were several opportunities to do so, e.g. the Open University, HNDs and HNCs. By chance he then came across this programme, which was very close to what he wanted. It was agreed as soon as he was appointed as apprentice that the employer would fund his continuing education. "…the agreement was that they would pay for my further development as far as I wanted to go" (00:02:39.1). He regards himself as a trainee or apprentice but these formal qualification pathways are not officially used in his company.

Matt is an electronics technician in a state-owned company. He started his training (*advanced apprenticeship*) here some years ago, studying at a *training college*. He originally wanted to progress directly on to continuing vocational education and training, but funding for continuing education and training was cut due to the recession. After a few years, he looked again at the available options. The course of study was recommended to him by a member of staff at his training college who had taken the course himself. Applying and obtaining consent from the company was a real balancing act for him. He visited the campus with his supervisor, and they found out about the content of the programme.

View of the companies

Employer 1 is a family business with approximately 100 employees. An apprentice was planning to complete a degree after his qualifying, but the company wished to keep him. "But we did not want him to go so we offered him the opportunity to do the higher apprenticeship" (00:02:38). This apprentice is now in the process of completing his bachelor's degree. Another *higher apprentice* has also been recruited, and he was also offered the opportunity "to go as far as he wanted to" (00:03:04). As a rule, *higher apprentices* are generally released for a total of around one day per week, and prior to the examinations the company is "quite generous with the time they are given" (00:12:44).

The company is very satisfied and benefits from the content delivered in the degree. A WBL project was selected in consultation with the lecturers which was of benefit to the company and which met the university's requirements.

Employer 2 is a government body. It supports its employees in obtaining higher-level qualifications because they are seen as a requirement for progressing within the company. "We would like everyone with any responsibility to be degree qualified" (00:11:34.1). For the company, a university degree demonstrates competence and the ability to learn.

---

44   *"College"*, probably a further education college.

It would be difficult to find exactly the right course due to the company's high level of specialism. The superior and the employee looked at the programme, and whatever the employee opted for was approved: "He's learning in general and, more specifically, what he needs for the rest of his working life, not just what we're doing here" (00:07:16.0).

Within the company, participants on the programme have the status of "sponsored student". There was some contact with the university, but the interview partner would have liked more.

Work-based learning

Matt had some problems in completing the WBL module. He had already been in his position for several years, which meant that it was difficult for him to find new areas. Since starting the degree, he has therefore already changed his position internally three times. One of the positions involved shift work, which meant that sometimes he had to attend the course straight after the shift. He had to study for university, become familiar with new jobs and also look around for new opportunities all at the same time. He found that very stressful. "And you know it's just ongoing slog" (00:08:35.7). He had originally assumed that the university offered courses, as needed, for the WBL. However, the content of the only course available was not right for him. He was a bit too late in setting about finding an opportunity to take an accredited course at the required level within the WBL module. It was then difficult to find appropriate courses at a sufficiently high level. The duration of potential courses was at least a year and would therefore have run beyond the time remaining on the foundation degree. He was also a little late in starting his final project – on the one hand because he had assumed a different time frame, and on the other because his company was a little inflexible. Simply gaining approval for the funding took a lot of time.

Matt has a supervisor in his company, but it was largely down to him to sort out his own training. He found that difficult.

The situation for Liam is entirely different. The work to be done in his company is so varied that he tends to be spoilt for choice. He has compiled a list of appropriate tasks or projects and decided together with his supervisor which of these would be of most benefit to him and the company. He has a completely free hand in terms of how these are carried out. He is under no pressure and works on his project when he has time for it: "As long I'm, you know, working to my potential right, I just sort of get left to do it" (00:17:37.5). For him, the project is a very good match for the tasks he does at work.

View of the training institution

The experience of the interview partners at the training institution indicates that the WBL is not implemented equally well in every workplace, as there are differences in the range of tasks and in the level required. For most students, completion of the WBL is not problematic and most also receive support from the employer. For the discussion partners, however, it is important in this respect that the WBL is part of the work and does not become a burden for the company. "...we want to capture learning that takes place at work and where you are developing and, and that shouldn't be a burden for the company or for the student" (00:16:08.2). The interview partners are therefore flexible and also facilitate tailored, personalised approaches whenever it makes sense to do so. The regular courses are specified by the university and must be taken, but the WBL gives students flexibility.

For the final project, details are also agreed with the supervisors in the workplace. This is assessed by the university and also includes the feedback from the company on satisfaction and goals achieved.

According to the experience of the interview partners, students are by and large supported by employers and given as much scope as possible. Some students are very fortunate. The higher apprentices from the large employer are, for example, released for exam preparation and are also given the opportunity to study during working time. However, this also impacts on their experience. "They're given a lot time at work to do university work. There's, it's a very supportive, possibly not realistic, experience that they're given." However, other students receive very little support. In very rare cases the employer expects, for example, that they work beforehand or afterwards on other days to make up for the time spent during the day at university. Some students – in particular in small businesses – are under a lot of pressure at work.

The training institution usually holds a meeting with the employers once a year. Although the "Industrial Board" enables employers to be involved in the design of the course of study, this does not relate to specific content. The interview partners are concerned that a greater focus on the employer in preparation of the content could move the programme towards the dividing line between education and training. "The risk if we were to move to more employer-led content [is that] we are getting close to the boundary between education and training" (00:28:14.7).

The programme is the only course of study leading to a *foundation degree* which is still conducted by the university itself. All other foundation degrees offered by the faculty are implemented under licence by a vocational college.

Satisfaction and outlook

Liam is very satisfied with the degree: "Love it, it's great. It really fits in well with what we do at work" (00:02:26.6). He would take the course again, because he can see no other realistic alternative for his planned career development. In this respect, it is important for him that the course is offered at the university. Liam regards it as a benefit that more self-initiative is demanded and that personal development is encouraged. For him, it is also an advantage that he completed relevant training beforehand. As a result, he finds a lot of things straightforward and is able to make connections, which means he is able to build on his existing knowledge. He also found the professional discussion with other participants very interesting.

Liam is grateful to his company and feels tied to his employer because it paid for the course. He has an agreement which specifies that he must repay part of the course costs if he leaves his employer within 12 months of the end of the course.

Liam's final goal is to obtain a bachelor degree. He regards a technician as an engineer without the university degree and his aim is "…to progress to a full engineer and move up the chain as high as possible" (00:05:03.2). He has already almost gone as far as he can go in terms of promotion opportunities in the engineering area and is primarily looking at the possibility that his salary will be increased. For him, the only opportunity for progression would be moving to management, but he is not looking to take this path.

Matt is also aiming to get a bachelor's degree. However, he is not sure whether he would choose the course again. He has a colleague who also completed a *foundation degree* at an *(FE) college*, however with significantly less work. "…so I'm kind of yes it's been good; […] I've made it more difficult for myself by applying for this course" (00:07:44.0). However, he feels that he has developed as a result of the course. He is grateful for the experience gained as a result of the moves within the company which the course required.

Matt has a contract tying him to his employer for two years following completion of the degree, but this does not increase his personal attachment to the company. His viewpoint is that he has worked very hard and that his company has already benefitted from his degree. He has promotion opportunities, but in his company the processes are very boring. In a couple of years' time, he is therefore planning to move into industry for a few years and could well imagine himself returning afterwards with new experience.

Conclusion

This case study shows how heavily dependent implementation of WBL is on general company conditions and the wide differences which exist between the study conditions of the individual students depending on the company. This is also reflected in the company interviews, which illustrate the varying motivation of the employers. We see an SME which is trying to retain a good member of staff and make the best possible use of the higher education study for the company. In the other example, the focus is merely on the title, whilst the course content plays a very subordinate role. The major company with several students offers its *higher apprentices* a structured company-based element of training and extensive support. By way of contrast, the spectrum of practices in the other companies is very large.

This case study also makes it easy to see how the *foundation degree* qualification has been marketed in a targeted way as a "better" alternative to the traditional higher education programmes of the HND and HNC. In times when large amounts of state funding were available, specific efforts were made to market the new qualification to employers, and almost all *foundation degrees* offered by the faculty have now been outsourced under licence to *FE colleges*.

3.3.2 Ireland

Case study 1: "Electrical Apprenticeship"

Overview of case study interviews

IE_St_CS1_1	Apprentice 1 – Aidan*
IE_St_CS1_2	Apprentice 2 – Kyle*
IE_C_CS1_1	Company 1 – a private-sector company with 400 to 500 employees plus approximately the same number of subcontractors
IE_C_CS1_2	Company 2 – a major public-sector company
IE_EI_CS1_1	Head of School IoT, Head of Apprenticeships IoT
IE_EI_CS1_2	Lecturer IoT
IE_EI_CS1_3	Assistant IoT
IE_M_CS1	Representative of SOLAS

*Names altered

Background information

At the time when the case study was conducted in 2015, there were 26 training occupations in Ireland subject to supervision by the *Further Education and Training Authority* (SOLAS). Nationally valid standards drawn up in conjunction with the social partners were in place for these training occupations (see IE_M_CS1). At the time of the case study, a revision of the curriculum for the training occupation of electrician was underway respectively had just been concluded.

The formal entry requirement to these training occupations is the Junior Certificate, which is acquired via a state school examination taken at a minimum age of 16 following the end of mandatory schooling. In practice, companies usually prefer young people entering training in the occupation of electrician to be in possession of the leaving certificate (IE_C_CS1_1, IE_C_CS1_2, IE_M_CS1). This is achieved by taking a second state school examination at the end of the upper secondary level.

In order to commence training, the apprentice concludes a contract with the company. Companies are required to register with SOLAS. A visit to the company takes place in order to check suitability to provide training (IE_M_CS1). The company providing training reports new apprentices to SOLAS. SOLAS employs training advisors who support both the companies and the appprentices and organise the implementation of the theoretical phases of training.

Training is of a minimum duration of four years and features alternating phases of practice and theory. The duration of the theory phases is stipulated, whilst minimum requirements apply to the length of the company-based practical phases.

Phase	Location	Duration (minimum)
1	Industry	20 weeks
2	Training centre	20 weeks
3	Industry	40 weeks
4	Institute of Technology	11 weeks
5	Industry	26 weeks
6	Institute of Technology	11 weeks
7	Industry	12 weeks

Apprentices spend the first phase of their training in the company. During the second phase, they complete a 20-week basic course at a training centre.[45] The two further theoretical phases (phase 4 and phase 6) usually take place at *Institutes of Technology* (IoTs), technical institutes of higher education run by the Irish state. The IoTs are commissioned and remunerated by SOLAS and thus act as service providers. Apprentices are allocated to the individual IoTs by SOLAS. Inclusion of the IoTs in training takes place for historical reasons, since some have emerged as successors of the old technical VET institutions.

Apprentices receive an allowance from their company during the practical phases of training. This is paid by SOLAS during the theoretical phases of training and is financed via a training levy and tax revenues (IE_M_CS1). Remuneration rises following successful completion of a phase (IE_C_CS1_1).

Successful conclusion of training leads to acquisition of the *Advanced Certificate Craft*, which is aligned to Level 6 of the national qualifications framework and to Level 5 of the EQF. In 2015, this alignment was confirmed following an investigation by *Quality and Qualifications Ireland* (QQI), which is responsible for the awarding of qualifications.

In 2015 and 2017, the Irish Government staged bidding rounds for new training occupations in other occupational fields and at higher levels of the national qualifications framework. Some of these new *apprenticeships* are now already being offered (see Chapter 3.2.2).

---

45 The training centres were originally run by the predecessor institution of SOLAS, although they now belong to the Education and Training Boards following institutional reform.

Because training is linked to a contract with a company, it is also dependent on the economic situation. A dramatic collapse in numbers of apprentices occurred in Ireland in the wake of the recession. The number of training contracts is now rising once more.

Evaluation focusing on the perspective of the apprentices

Aidan and Kyle are currently undergoing training in the occupation of electrician. Aidan is in phase 4 of his training, Kyle in phase 6. They are completing these two phases at an IoT.

Access

Aidan worked in mechanics after finishing school ("I was doing mechanics", 01:07) and gradually worked his way into the field of electronics. When he saw an advertisement for a training place as an electrician, he found out more about the sort of work involved and about opportunities for further development ("…on the types of gates that opens for you" 01:07). He enjoys working in electronics and is also good at it. He also notices that he needs professional prospects. After submitting his application, he was invited to attend an interview conducted by a senior manager and the Head of Human Resources.

Kyle, on the other hand, comes from a "family of electricians", and some of his friends are also in the trade. After completing his *leaving certificate*, he studied IT before spending a number of years doing casual work in the agricultural sector both in Ireland and abroad. Following a phase of reorientation, he took the decision to become an electrician too. This move was also based on a feeling that he had a good network in this area. His training place, or at least the opportunity to attend an interview, was facilitated via contacts.

Both began their training in a large company. Aidan estimates that about 22 or perhaps even more apprentices are employed in his company. Kyle thinks the number in his firm is around 60 to 80, although he is not sure.

Aidan entered the company providing his training in September 2013. After a sort of probationary period, training proper began in November 2013. He was registered at this point in time. He noticed this by the fact that he was paid the training allowance.

Company-based training

When Aidan's training officially began, various internal company training courses also started. Safety is accorded a major role, including in his contract with the company. A company training plan is in place. He completes a large number of internal courses, including a "Safe Pass Course" and grinding and flex training. He also receives smaller introductory sessions which depend on the requirements of the specific place of deployment. "If they have to get us trained up on it, they'll get us trained up on it…" (05:52). The company providing training further ensures that all the content necessary for the phases spent outside the company is imparted beforehand.

In order to support its apprentices, Aidan's company operates a "buddy" system in which an apprentice is assigned to a qualified electrician during orders. This also takes place for safety reasons. The duration of orders varies. Some may be for one day, but others extend over a whole week or even months. Sometimes only partial orders are completed, or the trainee is taken off the job and allocated to another order. Assignment to orders is guided by status of training, the requirements of the training plan and the needs at the order location. Distribution is usually coordinated by a human resources officer, although this function is sometimes performed by the relevant foreman on site. Each apprentice is assessed on a monthly basis. The foreman and the "buddy" come to the building site for this purpose and speak to the apprentice for around five minutes. They talk to him about his work, discipline and attitude and also address any critical points. They mostly have a form with them, and this is filled out with information such as tasks performed and attendance.

The situation at Kyle's company providing training is entirely different. "If you don't look after yourself, they don't look after you. So if you're not aware that you're not learning enough you get left behind" (04:44). Kyle is of the opinion that he has not yet worked enough with his hands. Although he is in phase 6 of the training, he has not yet been given any real responsibility. During the second year of training, he was on a very specialised construction site where he was able to assume some degree of responsibility, but the specialist nature of the environment meant that the skills he acquired were "not useful in the outside world" (06:14). In the third year of training, he specifically asked to be transferred to another building site, but here he also spent a lot of time performing the same activity. The workers were under considerable pressure, and there did not appear to be any time to give instruction to apprentices. He was allocated tasks with which he was already familiar and which he could complete quickly. With regard to fulfilment of the official requirements of SOLAS, his view is, "It's just a form that is signed" (06:21). He was not previously aware that quality assurance is in place for the practical part of the training. Neither does he receive any support. "And it's such a big company that it's so easy just to have one man in charge of the apprentices. And because of, because they don't really value their apprentices it's, it's so easy to swap them around, you know. If there's a first-year here and a first-year there, it makes no odds. This, the supervisor doesn't care which first-year he has because he's only doing monkey work anyway, so why not swap them? Yah, no I have a, a big issue with that" (07:13). Kyle is very frustrated with the situation, because the status of his knowledge is not at the level it should be at this stage of training. He plans to leave the company for the last phase of the training and intends to address his criticisms within the company even if he ends up staying. Some of the apprentices who complete their programme are taken on permanently if there is a human resources need. According to Kyle, there is no reason not to invest in the apprentices. This would enable them to be deployed more effectively in the later years of training and would also make better use of the electricians who had completed training and were now working in the company permanently.

View of the companies

The representatives of the two companies surveyed are both responsible for the coordination of training in their companies. In the case of company 2, the representative even fulfils this role on a full-time basis. Both companies set great store by good quality and varied training. For this purpose, they work with appropriate training plans and use the rotation principle. Firm 2 offers company-specific modules in addition to the stipulations of SOLAS. In both companies, apprentices are supported by the respective specialist line manager, and a buddy or mentor system has been established to provide assistance. Quality assurance of training plays an important role in both companies. Apprentices are required to have their "log book" signed and checked on a regular basis. This records details of contents completed. There are also frequent feedback meetings which focus both on professional assessment and on the conduct of the apprentices.

The representative of company 2 reports that all the content taught by the company is compiled in a list by SOLAS at the end of the training. On this basis, a meeting is held with SOLAS to discuss the list and to decide whether all content necessary for the awarding of the qualification has been included. The representative of the company takes part in these meetings.

Extra-company element of training

The assessment made by the apprentices of their first extra-company phase (phase 2) spent at the training centre is just as different as their views regarding the situation in the company. Aidan felt that the content he was taught during his six months at the training centre could have been imparted in ten weeks. Kyle, on the other hand, found this phase to be "brilliant" and thought his teacher was "fantastic", although he only spend about four-and-a-half weeks at the training centre because of holiday periods. Aidan felt that the second ten-week extra-company phase (phase 4) was much too short for the content taught, which he viewed as being considerably more challenging. Kyle, however, who already holds a higher education qualification, was satisfied with the length. When asked if he thought it would make a difference if phase 4 took place at a training centre or at an institute of technology (IoT), Aidan was clearly in favour of the IoT. He felt that because the lecturers at an IoT also teach full-time students they are also highly experienced with regard to the material to be taught and the courses to be completed.

Aidan remarked that he found some difficulty in making the switch back to "school mode". Intensity of work during phase 4 is very high. The apprentices attend the IoT between 9 am and 5 pm three days a week and from 9 am to 4 pm on Wednesday and 9 am to 1 pm on Friday. Although no homework is set, the apprentices are required to complete sample exercises. Aidan works on these in the library during his breaks. He adopts a very targeted approach in order to make use of the time and pass the four examinations at the end of phase 4. "Failing is not an option" (25:03). Phase 6, which Kyle is currently completing, also concludes with four examinations.

The apprentices are now required to pay registration fees of €1,000 to the IoT. Aidan's company supports its apprentices to the extent that it advances this money and then deducts it in instalments from the training allowance.

View of the Institute of Technology (IoT)

As far as the institute of technology is concerned, the theoretical phases represent an organisational challenge for those responsible since the blocks are often announced at very short notice by SOLAS. There is also a strong degree of dependence on SOLAS (IE_EI_CS1_3).

Most of the teachers on the programme have themselves completed training as an electrician and have the appropriate industrial experience. The lecturers interviewed believe that participation in the electrician training represents considerable added value for the institute because networking with the apprentices provides them with an insight into virtually all companies in the sector. They feel that these insights are very important, especially with regard to the quality of programmes delivered to full-time students (IE_EI_CS1_2).

The teachers also enjoy working with the apprentices because of the maturity they display. The apprentices generally work in a highly focused way, show good commitment and ask a lot of follow-up questions in order to ensure that they really understand the content. The institute provides the apprentices with active support in planning their further career pathway and offers them the opportunity to attend evening study courses or make the transition to full-time programmes of study. Attending the institute enables the apprentices to become familiar with the academic environment and with the teachers in particular. This makes it easier for them to opt for a further programme of study. At the same time, the institute is in this way able to acquire new and high-performing students (IE_EI_CS1_2, IE_EI_CS1_3).

At the time when the interviews were conducted, SOLAS was carrying out a pilot project in which phases 4 and 6 took place at a training centre. Amongst the institute staff interviewed, this gave rise to the fear that this model could be adopted in future because SOLAS and the training centres originated from a single institution and still operate in close proximity (IE_EI_CS1_3). The costs at the institute are also higher because lecturers hold higher education qualifications and are paid accordingly (IE_EI_CS1_1).

Satisfaction/outlook

For Aidan, the apprenticeship was not initially as he had expected. He needed to get used to things and also had to motivate himself. Nevertheless, he is glad that he chose this route because of the opportunities which will open up once he has achieved his qualification. "...because of the gates it can open for ya after you, you finish your apprenticeship. You can go on and do electrical engineering, environmental engineering, all that type of stuff..." (01:29).

When he has finished his training, Aidan intends to live and work abroad. He will specialise in the industrial sector. He assumes that all the content necessary for him to exercise his profession will be imparted during the apprenticeship. "...I hope that after four years that any, any work that we come across, that we'd be able maybe [to] take five, ten minutes to work it out, but we will be able to throw your hand to it or tackle it at some stage, yeah, definitely" (17:00). He has also not ruled out the idea of entering higher education, probably electrical engineering or environmental engineering, because these programmes relate to his apprenticeship in terms of content and he therefore believes he will find them easier.

Kyle does not wish to give up. He plans to spend his last year of training in a company owned by a family member where he will be able to learn quickly and gather as much experience as possible in order to arrive at a point where he feels "I'm at the right level" (10:51). After completing phase 4 in the previous year, he embarked upon an evening course in "Electrical Services Engineering" at the IoT and "can't imagine how you could study this stuff not being an electrician" (15:19). This year, he will complete a higher education qualification at Level 6 of the NQF (Level 5 EQF), the same level at which his apprenticeship ends. In two years' time, he plans to do a qualification at Level 7 NQF (Level 6 EQF). If all goes well, he will be in possession of an honours bachelor's degree at Level 8 NQF (Level 6 EQF) in a further three years. During phase 4 at the IoT, the apprentices received comprehensive information about the opportunity to study on an evening programme. "They tend to talk to us quite a bit about it" (16:35).

View of the companies and of staff at the Institute of Technology (IoT)

The revision of the curriculum which was taking place at the time of the interviews was being conducted by a steering group comprising representatives of the trade unions, the employers, the training centres, the IoTs and SOLAS (IE_M_CS1). The lecturers at the IoT remark that the employer side has expressed a wish for new equipment and new course content as part of this process. In order to accommodate this, however, the lecturers believe that either more time will be needed or other course content will have to be removed. There were also plans to introduce a "portfolio", in which the apprentices would record the milestones of their training. The lecturers take a critical view of this, particularly with regard to smaller companies.

Both company representatives are very satisfied with the structure and the training itself. The representative of company 1 expressed a wish for modern technologies to be more closely integrated into the standards. The representative of company 2 would welcome the establishment of a *Programme Committee* with delegates from all stakeholders such as major employers, apprentices, SOLAS and the educational establishments in order to facilitate discussion of planned changes and to avoid irritations.

Conclusion

For historical reasons, part of the theoretical training of electricians in Ireland takes place at institutions of higher education. This promotes permeability because apprentices come into direct contact with the opportunities afforded by a further programme of study after completion of training, either in the form of an evening course or on a full-time basis. The teachers at the IoTs also benefit from working with the apprentices and can pass on the knowledge they acquire of everyday working life to their regular students in so far as they are deployed on full-time programmes. In the example case study, courses were also used in a targeted way to acquire new students. The benefits for both sides would, however, disappear if all theoretical phases were to be held at the training centres like in the pilot project conducted. Nevertheless, implementing the theoretical phases constitutes a challenge for the IoTs because they are acting as training service providers and requirements differ from those of the regular teaching at the IoT.

In this case study, both the practical part of training and work-based learning are also highly dependent on the company and its corporate philosophy. The company providing training to one of the interviewees does not live up to its responsibilities and deceives the responsible authority regarding training content taught, whilst the other apprentice has enjoyed a very positive training experience.

Case study 2: "Information Technology Support Programme (ITS)" at the Galway-Mayo Institute of Technology (GMIT)

Overview of case study interviews

IE_St_CS2_1	Student 1 – John* (one day per week model)
IE_St_CS2_2	Students 2 and 3 – Fiona* and Peter* (block placement)
IE_C_CS2_1	Company 1 – public sector
IE_C_CS2_2	Company 2 – private sector (start-up)
IE_EI_CS2_1	Programme Head
IE_EI_CS2_2	Lecturer 1
IE_EI_CS2_3	Lecturer 2 (many years of experience in placement support)

*Names altered

Background information[46]

The programme

The Information Technology Support Programme (ITS) began in 1999. It was jointly developed by several Institutes of Technology (IoTs) and was originally aimed at persons working in the IT sector without a relevant qualification. The programme followed a model of six months of study at the IoT, a six-month company placement, six months of study and led to the qualification of *higher certificate* at Level 6 of the national qualifications framework (Level 5 EQF). It was offered outside the academic calendar, and allocation of places was made directly via the IoTs rather than by the *Central Applications Office (CAO)*. The curriculum was the same at all participating IoTs, and there was a selection of jointly developed models. The regular coordination meetings were ended in 2006, and responsibility for the programme of study was handed over to the individual IoTs.

46 Unless indicated otherwise, this information originates from interview IE_EI_CS2_1.

The ITS at the GMIT

In 2007, the programme was continued at the GMIT in its original form. The economic crisis meant that changes needed to be made from 2008 onwards because placements were no longer available. The practical element was shortened to three months, and the subsequent theoretical phase was extended accordingly. The paid placements also became unpaid. In addition, students were allowed to work on a project as an alternative to the practical placement or to carry out the placement on one day per week during the second study phase.

Approximately 24 to 32 students commence the programme of study each year, and there are about twice as many applications. Admission takes place directly via the institute of higher education. An interview attended by a company representative is conducted with all applicants. The only admission requirement for study applicants aged over 23 (*mature students*) is that they must pass the interview. School qualifications (*Leaving Certificate*) are taken into account in the case of younger applicants, and entry requirements are lower for a *Higher Certificate* than for an *ordinary bachelor's or honours bachelor's degree*.[47] The programme begins outside the academic calendar in January. About half of the curriculum comprises theory, whereas the other half is made up of practical work in laboratories (IE_EI_CS2_2). Once students have acquired the *Higher Certificate* after a period of 18 months, they may progress without access restriction to a one-year further programme of study leading to the qualification of *ordinary bachelor's degree* (Level 7 NFQ, Level 6 EQF) and subsequently go on to get an *honours bachelor's degree* (Level 8 NFQ, Level 6 EQF) after one more year. Most students obtain the *ordinary bachelor's degree*.

Recent years have seen a rise in the proportion of students aged over 23, who frequently use the programme to pursue retraining. Financing options are also in place for this purpose (e.g. the *Back to Education Allowance*). Many students leave the programme after the third year of study because they have found a job. This particularly applies if the economic situation is favourable. Only a few of these subsequently return to complete the fourth year and obtain an *honours bachelor's degree*. Parts of the programme are also offered in the form of evening courses. Some of those on the programme take advantage of this provision to complete individual courses which they need for their work.

Direct admission is a considerable advantage of the programme of study, and those responsible wish to retain this system. The programme is primarily used by students from the region. The range of prior learning displayed by the new students is very broad (see IE_EI_CS2_2).

Involvement of companies

The content of the programme of study is reviewed every five years by a committee formed for the purpose, which includes an employer representative. Feedback from other employers is obtained on a regular basis too. Changes are, however, also possible within this five-year period if companies approach lecturers with requests for amendments.

Good relations with local employers have been established over several years via the practical placements. Employers are invited to attend presentations and in some cases also offer company tours for the students. The placements also provide a vehicle via which lecturers are able to gain information regarding the status of technology in the companies.

---

47 Generally speaking, fewer points on the Leaving Certificate are required for admission to a Higher Certificate than for admission to a bachelor's programme of study.

Evaluation focusing on the perspective of the students

1. Block placement

Fiona and Peter are *mature students* who have completed the practical placement via a block model.

Access

Fiona had previously completed a vocational Level 5 *post-leaving certificate* in business studies and bookkeeping and then attempted to pursue a career in the police. Due to the unfavourable general conditions in this area and because she had always had an interest in the fields of communications and technologies, she was looking to make the shift into the IT sector and had therefore opted for this programme of study. The opportunity to complete a bachelor's qualification was the crucial aspect for her.

She found her admission interview to be a highly positive experience because she was able to obtain a better insight into the content and requirements of the course. This would not have been the case had she made a central application via the CAO.

Peter worked for a telecommunications company for many years, where he completed a technician qualification in the 1980s. This is, however, no longer recognised. For this reason, and in order to acquire a higher qualification, he opted for the programme of study.

The opportunity to obtain a bachelor's qualification was very important to him. He was highly attracted by the prospect of finding a job after completing the *Higher Certificate* and then completing a bachelor's degree at a later date. Peter also found his admission interview to be highly positive, and direct access was a very good option for him too.

Course of study

Fiona takes a very positive view of the practical alignment of the programme of study. "That is one thing I would say about this course, it is very practical and very hands-on and I find personally I learn better from doing as opposed to hearing or seeing" (27:30). Peter agrees and also very much welcomes the fact that there tend to be ongoing performance evaluations rather than written examinations.

Both are very satisfied with the course of study and the lecturers. The programme allows students to specialise in software development and multimedia (development of websites and e-commerce). Like the majority of their cohort, Fiona and Peter have opted for the multimedia specialism. Although Peter expected that specialising in software development would open up better labour market opportunities, he himself found this route too challenging. Fiona also felt that greater prior knowledge would have been necessary.

Time, form and duration of the practical placement

View of the educational establishment

All three lecturers interviewed are clearly in favour of the block model because it is most likely to provide students with an understanding of how the IT section of a company works (see IE_EI_CS2_1). IE_EI_CS2_2 rejects the one day per week model because he does not believe that it fulfils the requirements of a practical placement in the tertiary sector (see IE_EI_CS2_2). The projects require a great deal of work on the part of the lecturers and are considered to be an emergency solution. "While a project is good, you will never replicate all the learning outcomes in a project that you would get in the work placement" (IE_EI_CS2_1, 27:08).

Although the lecturers found a six-month block to be the most effective option, they do not currently view this as realistic because they believe that a paid placement would be necessary. It was not feasible to implement this at the time when the interviews were conducted.

Some of the lecturers do not see the time within the course of study at which the placement takes place as ideal, but still wish to retain the qualification of the *higher certificate*. This necessitates an earlier placement so that students who are not progressing to the bachelor's course can also gather practical experience during their programme of study. In its present form, the *higher certificate* offers the advantages that entry requirements are lower than for a bachelor's programme and that admission takes place directly via the institute of higher education rather than being subject to the CAO.

View of the companies

With regard to the models, employer 2 does not see the one day per week model following a one- to two-week block as constituting any kind of problem (see IE_C_CS2_2). Employer 1 does not view this as an option. He would find it difficult to manage both in terms of the task and the provision of support (see IE_C_CS2_1).

Both employers see the early point in time at which the placement takes place as being positive. Employer 1 even believes this to be highly important because it provides the students with a very good insight and thus enables them to acquire a better focus over subsequent years. He himself would have liked to have completed his practical placement at an early point in time (see IE_C_CS2_1). Employer 2 has completed the ITS programme. He found the course to be very intensive and at the time also viewed his placement as a welcome relief. "It gave me time to actually sit and settle in my own mind what I'd actually got to do" (IE_C_CS2_2, 00:22:16). He also sees it as an advantage that students are able to obtain a focus for the subsequent period of study. He thinks that the length of the placement, which is three months at the commencement of the programme of study, is right. However, he feels it is too short as a single placement for the whole of the course extending over a period of four years if students go on to complete the *ordinary bachelor's* and the *honours bachelor's course* after the *Higher Certificate*.

Placement

Both students view the block placement as a more favourable option compared to the "one day per week" model and a project.

They are ambivalent regarding the time at which the placement takes place. On the one hand, they have the feeling that six months of study does not equip them with sufficient knowledge to become directly involved in work in the company. On the other hand, they have learned a great deal during the placement and this has also been of benefit to the further course of the programme of study. Peter takes a similar view and emphasises the advantages for the second semester. "To have done it first-hand makes it a lot easier" (18:26). On the other hand, this also made the placement more stressful (Fiona).

Both found that it would be more advantageous for the employer and for the students to conduct the practical placement after the second year when the students had learned significantly more. They would also welcome an extension of the placement to six months.[48]

Fiona has completed a three-month block placement in public administration. She found the placement to be highly interesting and very beneficial. A plan was drawn up prior to the placement detailing what was to be achieved. She received support from a line manager and from a further manager who reported to the former. She was able to turn to either at any time for assistance, and one of the two managers always monitored her work progress. During her placement, the company changed its operating system. One aspect which she found particularly interesting was that the two line managers had very different ideas. This enabled her to become familiar with a range of approaches.

Peter also completed his placement in block form at a cloud solutions company located directly on the campus, and he was very satisfied. His mentor had also completed the programme of study and was "absolutely excellent" (18:26). He showed Peter his tasks and was always available as a contact in the event of any questions. Peter found it a challenge to be integrated into the daily work processes, but it was also a good experience for him.

During the practical placement, the students are required to keep a weekly report in which they reflect on what they have learned. Fiona found this to be a very good approach because it enabled her to refresh what she had learned. Students are also required to produce a final report on the placement as a whole. They were working on this at the time of the interviews, and the report needed to be submitted at the end of the semester. Both students would have wished for a little more support in regard to aspects such as expected content and formatting. They expect that they will receive this information when their classmates completed their placement via the "one day per week model". At the end of the module, all students give a fifteen minute presentation which is followed by a discussion.

Support for the placement

View of the educational establishment

A placement mentor is appointed from amongst the teaching staff at the ITS. He or she supports the students in the search for a work placement, clarifies the tasks, support and role of the students with the company providing the placement and provides information on the students' prior knowledge. There are no formal stipulations for the company, and only an informal agreement is reached. No contract is concluded. During the placement, the mentor carries out announced and unannounced company visits and also acts as contact in the event of conflicts. One of the mentors has designed a simple form which enables the company to report any dissatisfaction with the trainee.

Trainees keep a log book during the placement in which they describe tasks performed on a weekly basis. This is countersigned by the person supervising them in the company. They need to submit entries made in the log book to their mentor whilst the placement is ongoing. When the placement has been completed, the students write a report and make a presentation.

---

48 Both expect to obtain an *ordinary bachelor's* qualification. If the practical placement took place after the second year, this would mean that students only wishing to complete a Higher Certificate would not subsequently return to the GMIT.

The nominated teacher is allocated a certain period of time to look after the students completing the placement, although this frequently proves to be insufficient. Interview partner IE_EI_CS2_3 believes that there is a lack of institutional support for the task at hand, such as when problems occur. There is no preparation on how to deal with issues and no support in cases of conflict. The block placements also take place in summer, which means that any assistance in an emergency has to be given whilst the teacher is on holiday. One particular feature of the programme is that mentoring for the placement is provided by academic staff. Some years ago, administrative support was available. This system has, however, been cancelled and not replaced (IE_EI_CS2_3).

View of the companies

Employer 1 (IE_C_CS2_1) has been taking on students from the ITS programme of study for a number of years. His division has developed an internal process for the placement. Because students have highly differing levels of prior knowledge, the placement begins with very simple tasks. A few selected employees are in charge of inducting the placement students. These members of staff are quickly able to assess their prior knowledge. Students are supported by one main employee throughout and receive regular feedback (see IE_C_CS2_1).

The students learn a great deal during the placement, both about technology and with regard to social skills. All staff members are prepared to take time to explain things (see IE_C_CS2_1).

Employer 2 (IE_C_CS2_2) also takes the students' prior knowledge and strengths as a starting point. He offers an environment in which they can practise and try things out whilst also encouraging them to specialise in a certain area. He then attempts to teach them as much as possible in this field. A short briefing on the status of work is held each morning, during which questions relating to the previous day, any preferences of the students and upcoming tasks are clarified (see IE_C_CS2_2).

According to the statements made by the interview partners, only about five of their group of around 20 students have completed the block placement. Both believe that students must also be lucky enough to obtain a placement. Fiona and many of her classmates often did not receive any response to their applications. The students are also competing with the unemployed, for whom the government has put a funded six- to nine-month placement programme in place (*JobBridge Scheme*). Because of the longer duration of this measure, Peter believes that such applicants are more attractive for the companies. For this reason, they are also used to placements which do not cost anything.

Outlook

The two students agree that a bachelor's qualification is expected on the labour market. Both are therefore striving to achieve an *ordinary bachelor's*. Peter assumes that many of his classmates would be happy with this qualification and would then seek to find a job before perhaps subsequently being interested in pursuing an *honours bachelor's degree*. Because Peter is a *mature student,* he would like to enter the labour market as quickly as possible. Fiona adds that the IT sector is changing very rapidly and that it would make sense to complete further courses in a few years' time. She also remarks that "being mature usually means you have to get money, right?" (IE_St_CS2_2, 00:23:53.20).

2. One day per week model

John began the study programme upon leaving school and completed the placement on one day per week during the semester.

Entry

John originally wished to study digital media, but the marks in his *Leaving Certificate* meant that he did not fulfil the entry requirements for a programme of study leading to the honours degree. For cost reasons, he did not want to study too far away from home and began looking for options in the region once he had finished school. He came upon this particular course, to which he was very attracted because of its focus on computers. Starting in January meant that he had six months off, a circumstance which he very much welcomed. His interview took place in November, whereupon he received the news that he had passed. He selected multimedia as his specialism. His assumption from the outset was that he would go on to complete all four years of the programme in order to obtain an *honours degree* because he also believes that this will offer better opportunities on the labour market than a Higher Certificate.

Course of study

John is now in the third year of his studies and is very satisfied with the programme. He likes the style of teaching and particularly enjoys the many practical elements, which he prefers to theoretical input. He is also happy that he embarked upon this programme rather than studying for a degree in digital media as he originally intended.

John is the youngest in his cohort and the only person who commenced the programme of study directly upon completion of general schooling. He saw the first year-and-a-half leading to the Higher Certificate as "ground level". During this period, which also took place against the background of the highly varying prior learning of the participants, the basic principles were imparted.

His fear regarding the third and fourth years is that the theoretical element will be too great in his eyes. He would prefer a more practice-related approach. "I think practical experience is better than writing, like, a five-page essay or report on something like that" (09:26). Nevertheless, he is enjoying his studies and thinks that those responsible have chosen the best possible alignment of the programme in terms of the necessary content.

Placement

John is completing his placement via the "one day per week" model. Originally, he wished to complete a bock placement in the summer and had more or less made the arrangements to do so. However, he then went on holiday to Italy for several weeks. Upon his return, his family received a visit. All of this meant that he did not get around to organising his block placement. He therefore opted for the other type of model, a choice which had the added benefit of not eating into his holiday time.

He is completing his placement at a computer repair shop, which he attends every Friday. His father is the branch manager. If he had undertaken a block placement, this would have been in one of the company's other branches. John writes a weekly report on what he has done and learned on placement fridays. This is countersigned by his mentor in the company and by the person responsible for placement students in the programme of study.

He sees one advantage of the "one day per week" model as being that he is in "learning mode" anyway. This makes it easier to get up in the mornings than it would be during the holidays. However, he thinks that it is generally more difficult to secure a placement under this model because there is no fixed induction time over a period of several weeks. His view is that students need to know what is to be done and that the employer has to be able to trust him to complete tasks without having completed an induction period.

Outlook

John hopes "to do the full four years and get my piece of paper to throw at people and say hire me please" (00:00:45). He is open to working in any area of the IT sector. He does not have any specific goals in life, but he loves computers and would like his work to involve them. One possibility is that he could apply for a job in the company where he is doing his placement. "And if it's fixing computers or doing other things with computers, it's perfectly fine with me" (00:04:41).

Conclusion

The unique feature of this programme of study is direct access without a central applications procedure. Students aged over 23 who are interested in entering the programme are even admitted solely on the basis of an interview. They frequently use the course to persue retraining or further training. The admission barrier for persons aged under 23 is also lower than that faced for a bachelor's course of study because the *Higher Certificate* is the initial qualification pursued. The programme of study largely attracts students from the region, and there are established links with companies in which the practical placement can be completed. Nevertheless, including because of the economic situation, some students experience difficulties in finding a work placement.

The students also tend to view the Higher Certificate as a route to a bachelor's degree rather than as a qualification with value in its own right. They agree that a bachelor's qualification is necessary in order to obtain better opportunities on the labour market.

3.3.3　Austria

Case study 1: Dual programme of study "Smart Engineering"

Overview of interviews

Ö_ST	Student Lukas*
Ö_EI_2	The interview partners comprise a representative of the "Smart Engineering" programme of study at St. Pölten University of Applied Sciences and a representative of St. Pölten Higher Technical Academy (HTL).
Ö_C	Representative of a company. He is the Head of Training in his company.

*Name altered

Background information

Although dual programmes are not very widespread in Austria, they are certainly perceived as being an attractive form of higher education study at the educational policy level (see 3.2.3). They are offered at four universities of applied sciences in engineering or IT study programmes.

The "Smart Engineering" programme is available at the St. Pölten University of Applied Sciences and is of a duration of six or seven semesters, depending on which study concept is chosen. It is open to graduates of the higher technical academies (HTL) as well as to those who have completed programmes at a higher general school (AHS) or at a higher vocational school (BHS). Nevertheless, the prior learning of around 90% of the participants in this dual study programme is in a technical area (e.g. HTL, apprenticeship). Only around 10% have attended an AHS or BHS. A Bachelor of Science degree is awarded once all examinations have been passed.

Because HTL graduates make up a proportion of about 70% of the first-year intake, the institute of higher education works in close cooperation with the local HTL. This cooperation includes aspects such as cooperation of curricula and joint use of HTL premises such as laboratories and workshops. According to the interview partners, the students with an HTL qualification perceive the transition between the two education establishments to be fluid. The main reason for this is the fact that both the HTL and the Smart Engineering programme feature practical components. Students with an HTL background are also able to obtain credit transfers for many parts of their prior learning. This means that it is even possible to shorten the duration of study.

The programme contains numerous cooperation arrangements with companies in the manufacturing and service sectors. Before the first students arrive at the companies to complete their practical phases, the original declaration of intent will be converted into a cooperation agreement to ensure firm regulation of the relationship between the three parties (institute of higher education, company, student). The university of applied sciences affords the companies plenty of opportunity to exert an influence. The development phase of the study programme included workshops during which the companies and the heads of programme at the university of applied sciences joined forces to coordinate the structure and content of the course. Local policymakers also enjoyed a right of co-determination during the development process. Their representatives were impressed by the idea, and it proved possible to get the ministry responsible on board.

All parties involved recognised the potential offered by the programme to strengthen the local economy and to counter the migration of up-and-coming young skilled workers of the future away to the major cities. In order to facilitate the development of similar programmes of study in the future, the university of applied sciences has set up a platform entitled *Dual Higher Education Austria* together with *AQ Austria* (Austrian Agency for Quality Assurance and Accreditation). This platform provides recommendations to the ministry with the objective of creating a separate category under law for dual study programmes in higher education.

Demand seems to be in line with the expectations of all parties. Even in the first year, applications exceeded the number of study places available. According to the interview partner, this is highly unusual for a new programme of study. Such courses normally require a few years in order to become established on the market. An additional administrative staff member was also appointed in order to deal with coordination of the study programme and communication with the companies. The application procedure is similar to the employment recruitment process. Applicants are invited to an aptitude test followed by an interview.

Evaluation focusing on the perspective of the students

Lukas has just commenced the "Smart Engineering" programme at the university of applied sciences. He previously obtained an HTL qualification before completing his civilian service with the voluntary fire brigade. He then began working for his present employer, which s pecialises in IT support. His original plan had been to gather a few years of occupational experience before entering an engineering study programme at the Technical University of Vienna or studying media technology at the St. Pölten University of Applied Sciences. Instead of pursuing this direction, he became aware of the Smart Engineering programme being offered in St. Pölten whilst he was still working in the company and applied without further ado.

Reasons for entering the programme

Lukas's decision to opt for the dual study programme was crucially determined by a key experience at the HTL. Whilst working on his thesis (*Diplom*), he had a feeling that he had never sensed during previous school years. This was the notion that he was creating a practical benefit. In theory, companies could indeed apply the ideas which he had explored in his work. This fact made him clearly realise that he definitely did not wish to go down an exclusively theoretical educational pathway. Small learner groups (30 participants per year) and extensive support from all stakeholders (in the shape of allocated mentors) were additional factors which made the Smart Engineering programme appear so attractive. As an HTL graduate, he was also able to obtain a credit transfer for some aspects of his prior learning, thus enabling him to skip two semesters.

Fixed contractual arrangements are in place for all parties involved in the programme. A cooperation agreement is concluded between the university of applied sciences and the companies. This defines the cooperation in more precise terms, detailing aspects such as learning content, practical projects and assessment of the students. Students conclude a contract of employment or training contract with the cooperating company. Contractual arrangements with the university of applied sciences merely take the form of registration. This creates a kind of contractual "triangle" which binds the three parties together.

Organisation of the programme of study

The programme has been designed to take place at weekends. This means that students are able to work in their companies during the week whilst completing the study courses at the weekend (plus Thursday evenings). Students can negotiate individually with the company contact partners as to whether they continue to work during the week and for how many hours. Lukas took the decision to fix his weekly working time at 27 hours in order to gain sufficient free time for self-study. Each semester, two blocks of one week each are spent at the university of applied sciences. The real practical phases begin in the third semester. From this point onwards, students regularly spend two months at the university of applied sciences each semester followed by two months working on their practical project in the company. The sole purpose of the final month of the semester is to reflect upon the project at the university of applied sciences with their tutor. The mark awarded for the project is informed via an evaluation by the tutor at the university of applied sciences, by the mentor in the company and (to the smallest extent) by the student himself or herself.

Practical project

Every semester, project topics are stipulated in conjunction with the companies for students to complete during the practical phases. Each student has two mentors for his or her project, one from the university of applied sciences and one from the company (Ö_EI_2). Following completion, students discuss the course and result of the project with the latter by filling out a feedback form. Once back at the university of applied sciences, they engage in an extensive appraisal meeting with their tutor there. The feedback gathered is collated and evaluated at the university of applied sciences, a process which ultimately leads to the awarding of a project mark.

Lukas reports that students who, unlike him, have not organised cooperation between the company and the institute of higher education receive considerable support from the university of applied sciences in the search for a suitable company. Employer pitch days take place every year at which interested companies introduce themselves and are able to establish initial contact with students. Prior to entering the programme, students are not required to have already found a company where they can complete their practical phases. Within the first two semesters, the institute of higher education will attempt to allocate all students across the cooperating company depending on preferences and strengths.

In order to adapt the programme of study precisely to the needs of students, it may be completed in two different ways (Ö_EI_2). The first of these versions involves concluding the programme in the usual way over a period of six semesters. The practical projects are carried out during the semesters, and workload per semester is 30 ECTS (credit points). The second version extends over seven semesters, the last of which acts as an additional practice semester. The workload in this case is 25 ECTS per semester. The latter model is suitable for all students who have their own family or who have been working for a longer period of time and thus have a high degree of responsibility and a high workload. As usual, the programme concludes with a bachelor's dissertation. Students can complete their bachelor's thesis in four different ways:

1. Via a research project in the company

2. Via a research project at the institute of higher education.

3. At a foreign location of the company (providing such locations exist)

4. At an ERASMUS cooperation location of the institute of higher education

Support in the company

According to information provided by Ö_C, two students from the Smart Engineering programme came to the company to complete their practical projects in the first year of cooperation. During these phases, they receive remuneration and have the right to paid leave. These and further points are regulated in a type of contract of employment or training contract. Because of his experience in apprenticeships and coaching, the interview partner knows that supporting students in the practical phase initially involves additional expenditure. Nevertheless, he is certain that all participants derive a long-term benefit from this dual study programme. He is very positive about the company taking on students permanently once they have completed their qualifications. He explains that the practical phases in the company do not take place in accordance with a strict teaching plan. The university of applied sciences provides stipulations which govern in approximate terms how the phases should be conducted. The plan is for the students to assume regular tasks performed by the company for a certain proportion of the time. Notwithstanding this, all company participants are aware that the students cannot be perceived as fully fledged staff members and that they need sufficient time to pursue their studies. The rest of the time (the ratio of both units is clearly regulated beforehand) is available for working on the project. Students still receive a strong degree of guidance during the initial phases. Towards the end of the study period, they take on more tasks and act autonomously in completing projects.

Benefits of the programme of dual higher education study

Lukas sees the duality of his programme of study as a considerable privilege. On the one hand, he is a fully fledged student at a state university of applied sciences. By the same token, he is viewed in his company as a member of staff with equal status to other employees. In addition, his colleagues hold the knowledge he brings from the institute of higher education in great esteem. Despite his young age, they are grateful for his ideas and advice. This is a source of pride to him and gives him a sense of being a valuable part of the company's staff. The double workload which Lukas faces because of his study programme is also taken seriously, and he receives sufficient free time to attend courses and phases of learning at the institute of higher education.

Status of dual programmes of study in the educational system

According to the assessment of one interview partner (Ö_EI_2), dual programmes of higher education study are potential competitors for continuing vocational education and training programmes because they are aimed at the same target group. Provision is mainly directed at persons with vocational qualifications who are then afforded access to higher education. According to the interview partner, this trend is already clearly discernible on the training market. More and more young people are seeking to enter further training, and this is a development which is increasingly to the detriment of conventional training at the intermediate level. This is taking place despite increased efforts on the part of the chambers and public institutions to support "classical" further training. In addition, this trend is being reinforced by low-birth cohorts. The interview partner states that university of applied science graduates who have previously obtained an HTL qualification are highly popular on the labour market because of the many benefits they bring. Because of the practical element of their courses, they enter working life at an early stage. This means that they achieve high lifetime earnings and quickly gain occupational experience.

The interview partners (Ö_EI_2) are of the view that the dual study programmes deliver advantages to all parties involved and should therefore be expanded further. They believe that they could also be capable of export if other countries were to show an equal degree of commitment.

Satisfaction and student wishes for the future

Looking back, Lukas would once more opt for the Smart Engineering dual study programme. The institute of higher education sets considerable store by a good group feeling amongst the students, and the Programme Head also undertakes considerable efforts to create a sense of well-being amongst participants. Lukas's company also makes great endeavours to structure cooperation in such a way as to deliver as many benefits as possible for the students. He feels valued and supported by the company. The constant networking between both sides (the company and the institute of higher education) and ongoing attempts to coordinate the learning content in a suitable way also add to Lukas's positive perception of the dual programme.

Lukas's wish for the future is for a greater fostering of the awareness and acceptance of dual study programmes in the higher education area. He is aware that all parties involved, and the students in particular, need to work on time management for this type of educational programme. He believes that his later job opportunities will be very positive since graduates of the Smart Engineering programme will already have work experience. He thinks that there is a very good chance that he will go on to study for a master's degree at the same university of applied sciences once he has completed his bachelor's programme.

Conclusion

All parties involved emphasise the positive aspects of the cooperation and appreciate the link between occupational practice-related elements and academic education. However, a high workload is experienced by the students in particular because they need to fulfil the requirements of both the institute of higher education and the company. Nevertheless, the conclusion drawn by the student is positive in overall terms. He believes that his occupational experience in particular will provide good chances with regard to job prospects.

Cooperation from the point of view of the company representative

According to Ö_C, cooperation agreements are in place between the companies and the institute of higher education which govern all areas of responsibility and contents of training (e.g. stipulation of mentors at both institutions). The company also cooperates with the Technical University of Vienna and the University of Vienna. Although the collaboration between this company and the institute of higher education came about by chance, it was subsequently revealed to be a positive move. Ö_C and a number of other colleagues had been afforded the opportunity to take part in planning sessions at the institute of higher education together with representatives of other cooperating companies. Theoretical and practical learning content was coordinated during these meetings, and companies also had the chance to communicate their own individual requirements. The companies were now also exerting considerable influence on the study programme. Company feedback on various aspects is regularly requested, and the firms are also involved in student assessments.

Ö_C is very appreciative of the cooperation agreement with the institute of higher education and finds that the dual study programme is fully in tune with the times. He perceives a growing together between the academic and occupational worlds. His experience has been that increasing numbers of companies are seeking skilled workers with occupational experience. He believes that the Smart Engineering programme offers just this opportunity to its participants. Graduates of "regular" study programmes often lack soft skills such as time management, cost calculation abilities, creativity and the capacity to work autonomously. This programme allows companies to train workers who are a good match for them. He is also of the view that the practical phases deliver a higher degree of long-term learning success and enable students to align themselves better to the labour market whilst they are still studying.

Case study 2: Public Accountant qualification

Overview of interviews

Ö_EI_3	Group interview with representatives of the Accountancy Authority (BBH) and the Association of Austrian Chambers of Commerce and Industry (WKÖ) at both a regional and central level. The BBH is responsible for the accreditation of examinations, whilst one of the functions of the WKÖ is to provide preparatory courses.
Ö_EI_1	Individual interview with a representative of the Austrian Vocational Training Institute (BFI), which has close links to the chambers and also offers preparatory courses.
	No interviews were conducted with persons who had participated in or completed the vocational training or with companies.

Background information

The Public Accountant qualification (BBH) offered here is achieved via completion of the relevant specialist examination. No mandatory training is stipulated for entry to the specialist examination. The BBH qualification is higher-level training for bookkeepers. Knowledge and skills are primarily acquired via informal means, i.e. on the labour market. Some competences are obtained via the non-formal route (in the non-mandatory preparatory courses). A broad range of preparatory courses is available at adult education institutions. Although practical experience plays a major part in acquisition of the qualification, there is no systematic interlinking between practice and the learning content in the preparatory courses. The specialist examination, which is governed by the Law on Public Accountants, the Austrian Industrial Code and the training regulations for accountancy professions, is conducted by the body responsible for master craftsman training in the Austrian chambers of commerce and industry.

A state agency is responsible for accreditation of the examination leading to the qualification of Public Accountant. The criteria are thus statutorily stipulated. This means that this is a formal qualification which is not, however, considered to be part of the formal educational system.

Higher-level qualifications in Austria[49]

At the higher qualification levels (NQF 5 to 7), Austria has vocational qualifications which are deemed non-formal and lie outside the educational system. These include the master craftsman qualifications in the craft trades sector and qualifications at technical academies run by adult vocational training institutes ("WIFIs"). The latter offer two-year programmes which lead to senior clerk or technician qualifications. Initial vocational education and training and practical experience are usually the prerequisite for entry. The aim is to consolidate and/or achieve specialisation of existing occupational competences. The WIFI technical academy works in conjunction with companies to develop training content. The teaching staff include professional experts from the companies. The main focus is on project work and case studies which are directly related to practice. Some of these are conducted in the company. There are currently six specialist areas. These are applied information technology, automation engineering, manufacturing technology and production management, interior and spatial design, marketing and management, and media information technology and media design. The two-year technical academy replaces the part of the "technical area" of the examination for the *Berufsreifeprüfung* (admission requirement for institutes of higher education), the business licence examination and the trainer examination. However, because both of these programmes are considered to be non-formal education, they are not included in international educational statistics or else only taken partial account of.

Prospects after qualifying

The main purpose of the examination is to provide a foundation for self-employment. However, many people do not avail themselves of this privilege because they wish to continue in employment with their companies. This certificate affords them the opportunity to do so, and a further certificate also leads to greater chances on the labour market. "…I believe that 90 per cent do not enter self-employment" (Ö_EI_3, 83).

According to the information provided by one interview partner (Ö_EI_3), the typical educational career pathway is to proceed to an examination leading to the qualification of accountant (*Buchhalter/-in*) after approximately eighteen months of occupational experience. After a further three years, it is possible to sit the examination for the qualification of Public Accountant (*Bilanzbuchhalter/-in*). Practical experience plays an important role in this educational pathway.

Accountancy MSc

The WIFI,[50] which is also an important provider of BBH preparatory courses, enables those who have completed the BBH examination to progress to further training in the form of the "*Accountancy MSc*" master's programme. This is offered in conjunction with the Vienna University of Applied Sciences, which ensures the quality of the continuing training and awards

---

49   See also 3.2.3.
50   See also 3.2.3.

the degree of *Master of Science*. "This cooperation means that although the university of applied sciences provides the stamp, teaching takes place entirely at the respective WIFI locations. Cooperation agreements are in place to ensure this" (Ö_EI_3, 33).

The programme of study is shortened to two semesters if a Public Accountant examination has already been completed, because the main focus of the first year of study is on this specialist area.

This qualification is not a recognised higher education bachelor's degree (a so-called Bologna bachelor's degree). Students entering this master's programme have previously completed courses leading to the qualifications of Accountant and Public Accountant. A formal higher education entrance qualification is not required. The more professional experience a participant is able to show, the greater will be the credit transfer such a person is able to receive, i.e. the study period is shortened accordingly. Credit transfer can, however, also be given for higher education or foreign qualifications. Credit transfer is assessed individually on the basis of documentation submitted. This qualification does not offer connectivity to university programmes.

The value which can be attached to this form of advanced "academic" training is certainly questionable, apart from the acquisition of a title which is at least capable of creating mistaken ideas regarding status and recognition. The workload faced by learners is definitely considerable. They need to attend courses at the weekend and also have to write their "master's thesis". At the time of the interview, initial results of the study programme were still being awaited because the first courses were due to end. Nevertheless, one interview partner (Ö_EI_3) had already received initial feedback. This suggests that both the time demands and the writing of the final thesis were very difficult in some cases.

The course

About 50 to 60% of participants on the courses leading to the qualification of Public Accountant are sent by their companies, which pay all or some of the costs of the programme (Ö_EI_3, 123). These forms of continuing training are also used to re-enter working life after a break to start a family. However, the interview partner believes that requirements regarding the level of the programme are frequently underestimated.

Learning materials are developed for the respective programmes. It is important to ensure that these materials are updated, for example when tax law is amended. Coordination with the companies in this sector takes place on an annual basis. The script authors and trainers meet once a year for this purpose, and workshops are also staged. Otherwise, there is no formalised cooperation with companies and no current plans to seek this (Ö_EI_3).

The continuing training courses are taught by so-called trainers. These trainers come from various areas and branches (ministries, companies of various sizes, tax offices etc.). Trainers meet representatives of the WIFI Association once a year to discuss and adapt the scripts to the courses. It is very important to the training providers that their courses remain up to date at all times. Great store is also set by compliance with the philosophy of "by practice for practice". Internal advanced company training courses can also be held if there is a group of learners from one company. "We have a good reputation" (Ö_EI_3, 36).

Companies provide standardised feedback at the end of the course. The example of the occupation of "payroll accountant" (*Personalverrechner*) shows how important this feedback is. This is an area in which company requirements have changed significantly, and this needs to be reflected in the courses (Ö_EI_3, 128).

As soon as three Austrian federal states develop and introduce the same advanced professional training programmes via the WIFIs which exist in each state, Head Office in Vienna ensures that uniformity is in place across the country, i.e. so-called standard Austrian products are created (Ö_EI_3, 34).

The Vocational Training Institute (BFI)

The BFI (Ö_EI_1) often cooperates with trade and industry within the scope of its education and training provision. As an adult education institution which is focused on continuing and higher training, it is important for the BFI to offer provision which meets requirements and is in tune with the needs of the labour market. There are no dual training programmes which encompass alternating phases of theory and practice. The emphasis of the programmes is on imparting practical knowledge and skills rather than on including academic and research-oriented content. Relation to the labour market and direct usability in practice of what has been learned are both important. According to the interview partner, company structure is the main reason why there is virtually no dual provision at higher levels in Austria. The vast majority of companies in Austria belong to the smallest category of firm or else are small and medium-sized enterprises. Cooperation agreements are easier to enter into with larger companies.

The education and training provision of the BFI which leads to higher-level qualifications is viewed as being "post-secondary" rather than being categorised as "tertiary". However, the BFI also offers tertiary training programmes. It is a provider for universities of applied sciences at which bachelor's and master's programmes of study can be completed (often on an in-service basis). The BFI also has a Short Cycle Academy (SCA),[51] which is specifically aimed at persons not in possession of an initial vocational qualification who have failed to complete the study entry phase successfully. The SCA is a three-semester course which leads to the qualification of "Academic Business Manager".

From the point of view of the interview partner, there is a "vacuum" in Austria in the area of higher VET. There is a lack of short vocational training programmes which are also accessible to those who have not completed the upper secondary school leaving certificate or initial vocational education and training. Universities in Austria have a different focus (seeing themselves as providing vocational preparation), and the same applies in respect of the universities of applied sciences (although they were originally conceived as a shorter vocational training option in the tertiary sector). What is lacking is "short-cycle provision" which is also deemed to be tertiary. However, the present higher education legal situation does not permit the creation of relevant provision leading to an academic qualification, and this is particularly the case for non-higher education institutions (such as the BFI). Nevertheless, the interview partner believes that a strong trend towards academisation can be observed, such as in the healthcare sector where the intention in future is that nursing training will take place at universities of applied sciences.

From the point of view of the interview partner, the area above upper secondary level is also extremely heterogeneous. Up until secondary level, Austria has a highly structured and ordered educational system. After this comes a kind of "uncontrolled growth". In order to make education and training provision at post-secondary/tertiary level more visible, stronger co-ordination or closer cooperation between providers of adult education/continuing training would be useful, e.g. in the form of a "joint umbrella".

The expectation is that the NQF will create a certain level of dynamism to educational policy debate, such as with regard to the establishment of short-cycle programmes (within and outside institutes of higher education). The NQF could also bring about a change in attitude in respect of the reputation and acceptance of qualifications, regardless of where they have their

---

51   https://www.bildungaktuell.at/bildung/bfi-fh-berufsbezogene-akademische-ausbildung/008803/; accessed: 18.07.2018

institutional basis. If higher education and non-higher education qualifications are aligned to the same level, this should display equivalence.

Conclusion

The example of the Public Accountant qualification highlights the challenge Austria faces in making advanced vocational training visible and connective. Higher vocational education and training largely takes place outside the formal educational system and is detached from higher education. In order to maintain the attractiveness of the vocational training pathway leading from training in the secondary sector to higher qualification levels, a kind of auxiliary solution was developed via the WIFI technical academy. The signal sent out regarding the significance attached to vocational education and training can certainly be a questionable one if an attractive vocational qualification such as Public Accountant, which is aligned to Level 6 of the national qualifications framework (bachelor's level), has to be given added value in the form of an academic "add-on" which constitutes a non-recognised *Sc.Master* which does not offer connectivity.

The question arising is a similar one to that being posed in Germany. Does an additional academic element improve the attractiveness of higher vocational education and training, or should the strengths, practical relevance and practical proximity of VET be consolidated and highlighted as a particular value by going down the Swiss route to a certain extent?

3.3.4 France

Case study 1: DUT programme "Corporate and Administrative Management"/LP Programme "Chargé de clientèle"

Overview of interviews

F_St_CS1	Interview with two students, Claude and François*
F_EI_CS1	Interview with the deputy director of one of France's largest IUTs, which has 5,500 students, and with a teacher on the Licence Professionnelle programme, specialist area of management. The IUT is divided into 17 specialist areas at four locations and offers both DUT and LP programmes.
F_C_CS1	The interview partner is the Head of Training at a regional bank with 2,000 employees and 220 branches. It has 400 student interns per year. Some are from the secondary sector, but the main emphasis is on providing placements in the tertiary sector.

*Names altered

Background information

The two-year vocational and practice-oriented educational programmes which lead to a *Diplôme Universitaire de Technologie* (DUT) are considered to form part of higher education and are offered by the *Instituts Universitaires de Technologie* (IUTs). Students can go on to acquire a vocational bachelor's qualification by completing a one-year *Licence professionelle* (LP) programme, and this may also be followed by a master's programme. Both programmes are also offered in the form of an *apprentissage*.[52] The entry requirement is a *Baccalaureat,* of which

---

52 All educational programmes in France can be completed in the form of *apprentissages*. This type of learning resembles dual training in that it is organised in a way which involves switching between learning venues.

France has three types with three different main focuses. Even though the DUT programmes are also open to secondary school leavers who have completed a vocational or technical *Bacca-laureat* (Bac Pro or Bac Tec), 66.8% of DUT programme participants in 2015 were in posses-sion of a Bac Gen (31.1% held a Bach Tec and only 2.1% a Bac Pro), (MINISTÈRE DE L'ÉDUCA-TION NATIONALE DE L'ENSEIGNEMENT SUPÉRIEUR ET DE LA RECHERCHE (MENESR) 2017). The LP programme is also available to those who have completed a two-year vocationally qualifying *Brevet de Technicien Supérieur* (BTS) (see case study 2).

Claude and François have completed a DUT and have just gone on to commence a one-year LP programme entitled *Chargé de clientèle* (customer advice). Both have a general higher education entrance qualification (Baccalaureate general) and have completed the DUT pro-gramme in corporate and administrative management (GEA) in Toulouse.

Access

Claude became aware of the DUT programmes via a friend of his brother. He obtained informa-tion on the relevant provider, the IUT, by visiting an open day at which he spoke with students and teachers. This inspired him to embark upon this vocational course of study. He initially wished to pursue a DUT in the field of *marketing techniques* via the apprenticeship route. This was, however, only available in a city far from home. Nevertheless, he still decided to pursue the idea and was accepted onto the course, but failed to find a training place. His alternative was the DUT programme in GEA at the IUT in his home town.

François opted for the programme after a recommendation from the study advisor at his school.

Claude and François decided to enter a DUT programme rather than a bachelor's course at a university because the former is more practice-specific and features a stronger level of student support. There are regular examinations during the course instead of a single crucial final examination, and the learning groups are also significantly smaller. At the time when the interview was conducted during the first year of the DUT programme in GEA at the IUT, there were six learning groups. Each of these contained between 20 and 25 students, thus providing direct contact with the teaching staff.

Development of programme content

Interview partners F_EI_CS 1 explain that there were 24 National Pedagogic Committees (CPN) for developing course content for DUT programmes at the time when the interview was carried out (2015). These committees comprise specialists, company delegates and representatives from bodies such as the Cereq (Centre d'études et de recherches sur les qualifications), a research institute. DUT curricula are monitored, revised and redeveloped where necessary on a five-year cycle. They are valid across the country.

LP programmes are also each licensed for a five-year period, but in this case the IUTs exercise a more direct and more individual influence on content alignment. The aim is for this flexibility to allow greater consideration to be accorded to the needs of the labour market. At the IUT of the interview partners, an annual meeting takes place with experts in order to monitor the LP programmes. Cooperation arrangements between an IUT and companies in the area of the LP programmes further encompass teaching assignments, the arrangement of training places and practical placements as well as student projects. External experts are also involved in the execution of the final examination. Each faculty has its own points of contact in the companies, whilst the partners of the IUT as a whole tend to be larger bodies such as the employer organisations, trade unions or professional associations. The aim of the LP programmes is to achieve professional inte-gration of those who complete the qualification (F_EI_CS1_1, _2).

The internships

The DUT programme in the non-apprenticeship form stipulates a practical placement ("internship") of three weeks in the first year. This is followed by an internship of ten weeks during the second year of the course. Support from the IUT is provided in the form of an oral examination to accompany the first placement, whilst students are required to attend two meetings at the IUT within the scope of the second internship and also to write a report.

Claude experienced no difficulty in obtaining a placement. For the first-year internship, he secured a place in an insurance company in his home town. In order to achieve this, he submitted an application and attended an interview. He found a bank, also in his home town, where he was able to complete his second-year internship. This contact also further enabled him to obtain summer jobs in each of the subsequent two years to earn money to cover some of his rent.

François also quickly succeeded in finding a placement. He sent out his CV to a bank together with a personal statement and secured his internship following an interview with the manager. He thinks it might have been helpful for him that he knew a bank advisor.

The two students have also found practical placements for the LP programme they are currently completing. These are of a duration of four months. Both receive € 400 a month, Claude in an insurance company and François in a bank. The IUT helps with the finding of placements by maintaining contacts with former students and companies in the region. During their internship, students complete a study project. The topics for these projects are agreed before the practical phases commence. Proposals mostly come from the companies and offer students their first opportunity to gain hands-on experience (F_EI_CS 1).

Claude has already been deployed across all areas of the insurance company. He has, for example, worked in the customer advice section where he has had direct contact with customers. He has also been involved in preparing offers and has worked at reception. To begin with, he was managed and supported by a staff member before going on to complete tasks on his own and autonomously. François started out in the reception area at the bank, where he was assigned simple tasks. These activities subsequently became more demanding and diverse, and were expanded to include areas such as mortgages. François became increasingly autonomous. Both students felt that they received good support from their companies and that their colleagues were very helpful. There were never any problems about asking questions, and help was quickly given.

According to the information provided by the IUT interview partners, both the company and the IUT make a contact available during the internship. There are two feedback meetings during the four-month placement, at which the writing of the project report is also discussed. This thesis must then also be defended in an examination.

Apprentissage

François applied for an *apprentissage* for the LP programme in order to be able to earn money whilst studying. He was, however, unable to secure a place. He finds this form of study to be more attractive because he believes that it results in a better understanding of the occupation. Claude, on the other hand, made no attempt to apply for an *apprentissage*. He had sought to go down this route for the DUT programme but was unsuccessful because the placement was a long way from his home and he had been somewhat too late in submitting his application.

The particular reason why places are limited is the differing degree of willingness and capacity of regions to finance such training. *Apprentissages* are subsidised via tax breaks, via exemptions from social levies and in some cases via direct state support (CHARRAUD 2016).

If the programme is completed in the form of an *apprentissage*, students keep a digital notebook in which they document the competencies and skills acquired in each section of the training. They receive support from two tutors, one from the company and the other from the IUT. During the IUT phases, students organise meetings at which they network about their experiences. The National Education Council stipulates which units of the curriculum take place in the company and which are imparted at the IUT (F_EI_CS1_1, _2).

The interview partners from the IUT explain that they have never as yet had to turn away applicants for an apprenticeship within their capacity as an educational establishment within the scope of the LP programme. Demand is too low. The necessary *apprentissage* places in the companies are often located in other towns and cities, far away from where the students live (F_EI_CS1_1, _2). In general, the number of *apprentissage* places supported by the IUTs varies from institute to institute. Some IUTs, such as the IUT in Lyon, have decided to increase the number of places significantly, but only for the second year of the DUT programme. The interview partners believe that the reasons for the weak student demand are a previous lack of esteem on the part of parents and the fact that students view the point in time as being too early in their higher education to go into practice and work. This assessment contrasts somewhat with the views expressed by the two students. At the same time, however, they perceive a growing interest in the LP programmes compared to the general university bachelor's courses of study. The crisis on the labour market has caused many parents to undertake a rethink. They are adopting an increasingly sceptical opinion of traditional study programmes and are holding the practice- and occupation- related LP programmes in ever greater regard.

Students in both groups, i.e. those learning via the traditional form and those completing apprenticeship training, currently study in joint classes at the IUT. One interview partner from the IUT believes that the organisation of these common learning groups is a major challenge because of the different times at which students are present.

The interview partners from the educational establishment hear very few complaints from the companies. There are no problems with the major firms at all, although smaller bodies such as NGOs may have an issue because the students are not paid and it is more difficult to organise work. In overall terms, things are slightly more difficult in the DUT programme. One clear reason for this is that student numbers are larger, 300 in each course as opposed to 25 in an LP programme. The latter figure makes everything clearer and easier to define. DUT students generally tend to complain more frequently than their LP counterparts, because they are less mature and less motivated to learn.

According to the interview partners (F_EI_CS1), companies are more likely to offer an *apprentissage* to LP students than to DUT students because they are interested in offering the former permanent employment and see this process as a kind of "pre-recruitment". A very high percentage of DUT students ("90%") go on to an LP programme. The DUT programmes are also viewed as being too general, whereas the LP programmes are thought to be highly technical and occupationally specific. The companies see this as delivering a greater benefit.

Evaluation of interview with the representative of a company about the practical placement and *apprentissage*

The company also offers *apprentissages*, albeit for LP programmes only because DUT students are not yet sufficiently specialised. They no longer offer these to BTS students because experience has shown that they lack the necessary maturity.

The company views the placements and *apprentissages* as a recruitment instrument for future employees. 20 to 30% of all newly recruited staff have completed a placement or *apprentissage* in the firm. Nevertheless, the company also sees taking interns as part of its social responsibility role. The bank takes on five or six students from the *Chargé de Clientèle* LP programme being studied by Claude and François (20% of the students on this course). In the year of the interview (2015), the bank had 15 LP apprentices and four master's apprentices.

Consideration ist being given to whether the number of *apprentissage* places should be increased and the number of practical placements decreased. The cost factor plays a part in this regard. Interns are also paid (see students), but are probably not subsidised.

The interview partner believes that the project work at the end of the LP programme does not deliver any added technical value for the company. He cannot, for example, report on any know-how transfer via the students. Although the bank does not have any formal cooperation agreement in place with education and training providers in the region, four or five of its staff act as teachers at IUTs. This gives rise to contacts and informal collaboration. The interview partner himself is one of the teaching staff but does not hold any additional pedagogical qualification.

F_C_CS1 evaluates the LP programmes as being very good in terms of vocational preparation. He is, however, of the view that the institutes of higher education take too little account of the changing professional requirements in the banking sector and do not develop sufficient relevant content. He expresses a wish for more genuine dialogue between the banks and the institutes of higher education.

Satisfaction

Claude really enjoyed his time in the company. He learned about the difference between banking and insurance and discovered his interest in the former sector. He subsequently opted for the LP programme in customer advice (*Chargé de clientèle*). Nevertheless, the content of his placement did not assist him with the subjects covered by his study course, because his DUT programme in corporate and administrative management (GEA) did not include any bank-specific but more general content. He would like to see a change in this regard, because he realised that his classmates on the LP programme who had previously completed a BTS qualification enjoyed advantages by dint of having studied bank-specific subjects. To this extent, the LP programme is comparatively more difficult for him.

François does not know whether he would opt for a DUT programme again, even if it did not turn out to be a bad choice. He had expected the programme to include more technical and occupationally specific input from professionals and practitioners. The fact is that the teaching staff on the DUT programme comprises 50% practitioners and 50% traditional teachers. He is also of the opinion that the teaching of English is too theoretical and not sufficiently practice-oriented so as to lead to greater fluency in the language.

Claude believes that he would enter work upon completion of the LP programme if he were to receive an offer of employment from his insurance company. Alternatively, he is planning to pursue a vocational master's qualification in the area of insurance and banking. The local university offers the possibility of making the transition from an LP to a master's study course in this area. There are three ways of going about this. Students can study at the university itself, at its affiliated business school or at the Institute for Business Administration (IAE) at the university. Claude's preference would be to complete the master's at the IAE in the form of an *apprentissage*.

François is also seeking to commence a master's study programme, but has excluded the possibility of directly entering work at a bank following the end of the LP programme.

Conclusion

The students appreciate the practice-related nature of the DUT/LP programmes and the practical experience they gain and would even have wished for greater emphasis in this regard. Both were interested in apprenticeships, but this was not possible due to a lack of provision in their region. Such provision is heavily dependent on the funding of these training places, both at the IUTs and the company interviewed. The cost factor is a crucial aspect for the company, and is weighed against the benefit of easier recruitment.

Case study 2: BTS programme "Banking"

Overview of interviews

F_St_CS2	Interview with two students on the BTS programme, Natalie and Jerome*
F_EI_CS2	Interview with the head teacher of a lycée. The head teacher also teaches on the BTS programme "Banking".
F_C_CS2	This interview partner has been manager of a small bank branch with four members of staff for four years.

*Names altered

Background information

The two-year practice-oriented educational programmes leading to a *Brevet de Technicien Supérieur (BTS)* are offered by various educational establishments, by the *Sections de techniciens supérieurs (IST)* and in particular by the *lycées*, whose fundamental focus is on secondary education programmes. Even though BTS programmes are also offered at non-higher education institutes, they are considered within the educational system in France to be tertiary and a form of higher education. Like students who gain a DUT qualification, those who complete a BTS programme have access to an LP programme (vocational bachelor). The BTS programme may also be completed in the form of an *apprentissage*. The entry requirement is a *Baccalaureat*. The BTS and DUT are aligned to the same level of the French Qualifications Framework.[53]

The BTS "Banking" programme was developed on the initiative of the banks and offered for the first time in the year 2000. It was initially aligned in a highly technical way and was less business-oriented before being revised accordingly in 2014. Since this time bank-specific Internet activities have also formed part of the programme. In the predecessor programme, students spent one day a week in the company and four days at the educational establishment (F_EI_CS2). The regular programme now stipulates block placements of three and five weeks, respectively, during the first year, followed by a further five-week placement in the second year.

The curriculum is developed by a committee, on which the banks are represented. The examination boards also have practitioner representation, in particular for the oral examination.

BTS places are awarded via a central database (APB, *Admission post-bac*). At the *lycée* forming the object of the case study, 1,200 applications were received for 35 places. The best 100 candidates were selected to take part in a second round. According to the representative of the *lycée*, the centralised application process leads to an anonymisation of applications and does not leave enough scope for individual interviews.

---

53 For further information, see HIPPACH-SCHNEIDER, SCHNEIDER (2015), HIPPACH-SCHNEIDER, SCHNEIDER (2017).

Evaluation focusing on the perspective of the students

Natalie and Jerome are completing a two-year vocational preparation and qualifying BTS programme at a *lycée*.

Access

After completing her *Baccalaureat*, Natalie attended a preparatory class at a military school before subsequently dropping out. She also dropped out of a BTS programme in bookkeeping and management (*Comptabilité et gestion*) after being unable to find an apprenticeship place. She switched to the BTS programme in Banking (*Banque*) and is studying the normal course, i.e. with practical placements. It was never her wish to pursue such a course because she does not believe that a BTS qualification will be very helpful to her on the labour market. She also does not find the programme to be particularly "vocational". She learned of the BTS programme because she had completed her secondary education at the same school.

After obtaining his *Baccalaureat*, Jerome began to study law. He found the course interesting. However, after a year, he began to wonder what he would do with such a qualification on the labour market. He thought that the programme of study was too general. For this reason, he looked online for a more vocation-oriented programme and opted for the BTS programme in Banking.

Internships

Three practical placements are completed within the scope of BTS programmes not involving an *apprentissage*. One of these is for three weeks, and two are of a duration of five weeks.

Neither interview partner was able to find a placement easily and quickly. Natalie needed the help of her teacher to obtain her first placement, but had difficulty in coordinating this with the working times in her casual jobs. She found her second placement herself, although this was at a different bank.

Jerome applied to bank branches in the surrounding area by submitting his CV and a covering letter. Payment during the placements depends on the approach adopted by the respective bank. Natalie explains that the bank at which she undertook her second placement only pays interns who are there for longer than four weeks.

Because the bank branch at which Jerome was completing his placement was so small, he received direct support from the manager, who holds a master's qualification. He dealt with a wide range of smaller tasks and was able to work autonomously to a large extent. However, he increasingly became embroiled in technical issues such as insurance policies and the granting of credits even if he had not worked on such matters in tandem beforehand. He believes that a certain degree of maturity is required to be able to complete tasks assigned during the practical placement. Both students felt that they were treated like normal employees during their placements.

During her second placement, Natalie was given a greater opportunity to say what she would like to work on. The bank at which she had completed her first placement had adopted a more regimented approach.

View of the training institution

According to the experience of F_EI_CS2, cooperation with the banks has become more difficult since they have been required to pay interns whose placement lasts for longer than 40 days. They avoid this situation by offering shorter placements. This forces students to complete a greater number of placements in order to achieve the stipulated overall time of 14 weeks. Private banks do not offer placements to BTS students. Any internships provided are given to ISCED Level 6 students, such as those on an LP programme. By way of contrast, experience with cooperative banks has been good. A network is, for example, in place with Crédit Mutuel. This is the result of individual commitment by teaching staff. There are no systematic cooperation agreements with companies.

Students usually find placements for themselves, otherwise they are assisted by the school. When making their applications, students receive particular support with tasks such as drawing up a CV.

During the practical placements, students keep a *skills notebook*, which is structured in accordance with the ten most important skills (F_EI_CS2). A similar instrument is also used by the *apprentices*. The notebook helps students to see which occupational tasks are facilitated by learning the skills required. According to the teacher, it is not easy for the students to acquire all ten skills necessary during the practical placement. If they fail to do this, it becomes difficult to pass the examination. The teacher visits the students during every phase of the practical placement and tries to monitor acquisition of the skills together with the company contact.

F_EI_CS 2 regrets the move towards block placements. She felt that the previous regulation, which stipulated that one day per week should be spent in the company, was more beneficial for the students. This coincides with the assessment given by the interview partner from the bank.

View of the company

The branch has provided placements for BTS programmes (BTS Banking or BTS Negotiation) since it was founded. It offers one place per year, sometimes two (F_C_CS2). Regular contact takes place with the school, although no contractual arrangements are in place. Most interns come from this school. However, applicants from other establishments have also been taken on. The bank to which the branch belongs pursues the objective of making itself visible to customers, hence the establishment of small branches. The offering of practical placements also forms part of this concept. The primary focus is not on the recruitment of future staff. Despite this, the branch offered employment to a former intern in the year prior to the interview. The current strategy of the parent bank is to offer students completing the BTS programme a so-called *Contrat de professionalisation* for a term of 16 months i.e. a contract on further education and training, leading to a recognised qualification, a form of apprenticeship.

During the placement, the company prepares a summary report of the activities carried out by the intern and of the conditions in which he or she has worked. All staff members at the small branch provide support. There is no specific area of responsibility with regard to the supervision of interns.

Students are initially deployed at reception and then go on to work in various areas depending on the competences they display. In overall terms, the company is satisfied with the interns. This depends on the level of commitment and professional understanding shown. Interns used to attend the company on one day per week rather than in blocks of three, four or five weeks' duration. This is seen to be better both for the company and for the interns themselves.

The bank uses its placements to try to exert a stronger influence on curriculum in terms of making it more practice-relevant (F_C_CS2). It is generally in favour of greater involvement of companies in vocational education and training because it strongly believes that "day-by-day" experience is needed in order to learn a profession in the banking sector.

Satisfaction and outlook

Both students are satisfied with their placements because they were given the opportunity to apply learning they had acquired at the educational establishment. Jerome even believes that the general knowledge he gained at school has enabled him to achieve a better understanding of the banking sector.

Natalie, on the other hand, is somewhat disappointed with banking. She thinks that there is too much emphasis on making money and transacting business and not enough of a focus on providing genuine advice in the interest of the customers. For this reason, she would like to move into the area of client guidance if she remains in banking but does not as yet have any specific notion of how she may pursue this. She hopes that she will find her specialisation during the master's programme of study.

Jerome would have liked to have been more involved in actual bank business during his placements. Instead of this, his areas of deployment included the sale of telephones and fire alarm devices.

Both would opt for a BTS programme again because they found the course to be very practice- and occupation-related. They see this as being very useful, and this approach has also helped them to identify their future education and training pathway. Having already dropped out of two other programmes, Natalie has found the motivation to carry on.

View of the educational establishment

One third of those completing the BTS Banque programme go on to work for a bank. A further third goes on to a further educational programme, and the remaining third does not wish to enter the banking sector (F_EI_CS2).

Because of the large areas of overlap, subsequent LP programmes are not of interest to students who gain a BTS qualification. This also leads to dropouts, because such courses are simply boring for those who have completed a BTS. Students do not experience any problems in adapting to their occupation or company after finishing training.

Conclusion

The BTS students interviewed appreciate the programme's practical orientation but are ambivalent about their experiences during the practical placement phases. Compared to students in DUT and LP programmes, it is even more difficult for them, and indeed virtually impossible, to obtain paid company-based training places in the form of *apprentissages*. Both the educational establishments and the companies tend to view the organisation of the practical placements in blocks as being problematic and disadvantageous. By way of contrast, they believe that switching learning venues during the week facilitates integration of the interns into the company. Experience gained during the practical placements has helped them to specify their occupational plans more precisely.

3.3.5 Norway

Case study 1: The "Y-veien (Y-Way)" bachelor's programme of study model at Telemark University College

Overview of interviews

NO_ST_CS1	Students Oliver and Adrian*
NO_EI_CS1	*Telemark University College*
NO_C1	The interview partner is the co-owner and manager of a company which employs 90 staff. Since 1992, the firm has been working in the field of planning and management of electronic installations in buildings, in trains and within the general infrastructure in Norway.
INO_C4	The interview partner works for a company operating 28 power stations which generate 3,000 gigawatt hours per year. It employs 115 staff at its main site and has partnerships in place with 20 further hydroelectric power plants. He also works as a lecturer at the university college.

*Names altered

Background information

Since 2002, an innovative study model has been in place in some bachelor's programmes and in engineering study courses in particular. It facilitates entry for interested persons who are not in possession of a conventional higher education entrance qualification and leads to a bachelor's degree via a specially adapted programme. This route is the so-called *Y-veien (Y-Way)*. The usual educational pathway into the higher education sector is via a relevant general secondary qualification or via a vocational qualification plus completion of a supplementary year. By way of contrast, the so-called *the Y-veien* enables those who hold a relevant vocational qualification to gain direct access to the *university colleges* in Norway. The *Telemark University College* was the initiator of this bachelor's model and became the first institute of higher education to pilot the programme it had developed. Although the *Y-veien* programme leads to a conventional bachelor's degree, the first-year subjects taken by students with a vocational qualification are varied in accordance with their existing competencies. In some cases, the two groups of students learn in separate courses during the first and second semesters, e.g. electronics or mathematics. A second-year course in mathematics is, for example, also amalgamated with a first-year course so that students with more experience are able to assist new students (NO_ST_CS1). In the third year, students are once again taught together. Within the scope of the European Qualifications Framework, the programme is aligned to Level 6.

The average prior work experience of students on the *Y-veien* model following acquisition of their vocational qualification, the trade certificate, is two years (NO_EI_CS1). No company-based practical phases are stipulated during the programme itself. During the final year of study, students complete a specific company-related project. The problems or questions to be tackled are supplied by the companies. Students can also select the topic for their bachelor's thesis from this pool. The project phase is of a duration of approximately six months, and support is provided by a supervisor from the company and a supervisor from the university college.

Evaluation focusing on the perspective of the students

At the time of the interview, Oliver and Adrian were in the last year of the *Y-veien* programme of study.

Access

Prior to commencing the programme of study, Oliver had spent ten years working as an electrician in a company producing safety tools for electricians. He found the university college via his own research. It would have been possible for him to enter two other institutes of higher education, but he would have needed to complete an additional summer course in mathematics. His relevant vocational training and occupational experience enabled him to gain access to the bachelor's course of study at *Telemark University College* via the *Y-veien* programme. From Oliver's point of view, one further benefit of selecting this college is that he was able to pursue a specialisation in electrical energy.

Adrian had worked as an electrician in the Norwegian army for ten years. He opted for the university college on the basis of its good reputation and following the recommendation of acquaintances who had also attended.

For Adrian and Oliver, the study programme opens up an opportunity to explore various directions in engineering because jobs differ only in terms of small partial aspects. It is also possible to progress to a master's course of study. Adrian preferred to attend a university college rather than a *fagskole*[54] because he wished to achieve a more general qualification instead of a specialist certificate. He would have found it better if he could have commenced the study programme two years ago or even earlier. It had been several years since he had completed his electrician training, and the theoretical content taught by the school were no longer up to date.

The programme

Because they had many years of occupational experience, Oliver and Adrian found it easy to link specialist and technical learning content with practice during the initial semesters. For this reason, Adrian was able to skip part of the basic courses in electronics. Most of their fellow students on the bachelor's programme of study are significantly younger and have virtually no occupational experience. Adrian and Oliver think that it is more difficult for younger students in the programme to learn the technical and specialist content because they largely lack the ability to relate these to practice and are therefore unable to create a link between theory and practice.

However, Oliver also remarked that it is impossible to learn all the content of the study programme on the basis of previous occupational experience. In the fourth semester, Oliver experienced some difficulties in the subjects of chemistry, physics and mathematics. He personally perceives the period of study to be very long because he is no longer used to "sitting at a school desk". In his study subject, the latest technology needs to be learned and applied at all times. He fully appreciates this, although he also sees it as a particular challenge and circumstance within his study specialism. In his view, this is a significant difference compared to subjects such as economics or law. It is simply not enough to learn "old material" (97).

Most students finance their studies from their savings or from money they have put aside for the purpose. Although student loans are easy to obtain in Norway, the amount of money available is insufficient to fund a programme of study. Students do not receive any financial support from the firms in connection with their company-related projects.

---

54 With regard to the *fagskole*, see the second case study for Norway.

Cooperation with the companies

Some employees of NO_C1 work as lecturers in a number of subject areas in the engineering study programme. Company problems and issues are used by students within their projects or as the basis for bachelor's and master's theses. Some of this work takes place in the company, where supervision and support are provided. The company itself describes this as a practice placement, which lasts between three (bachelor's) and six (master's) months. An agreement is concluded between the company and the student for this type of placement. The company offers this in order to get to know the students with a view to later recruitment. One example of a current thesis topic is sun collectors in electric cars (NO_C1).

NO_C4 also cooperates with the university college. This interview partner regularly supports small groups of students with exercises and within the scope of their final projects. The interview partner sees benefits for the company by dint of the fact that processing of the company problems and issues by the students leads to the emergence of new ideas and because continuous contact is maintained with the university college and its lecturers. An exchange of knowledge takes place.

The interview partner (NO_C1) appreciates the cooperation with the *fagskoles* and the university colleges in general because students are able to demonstrate both higher education and practical experience. Nevertheless, the learning content of the master's study programme is very broad. In his experience, this makes it more difficult for the companies to find appropriate graduates. The company does not receive any state funding for its commitment to the programme.

NO_C4 likes to recruit *Y-veien* students, who are in possession of very good practical knowledge despite not being the best engineers in technical terms. They are familiar with the specific objectives of the company because of the practical experience they have gained as electricians. This increases motivation to expand technical knowledge. He believes that mixing them with university engineers is very good for the company.

NO_C1 hopes for more direct dialogue between companies and educational establishments in future. If there is closer cooperation, the interview partners believe that student placements could be extended and paid. One further prerequisite in this regard would be the ability of the companies to choose the students themselves.

NO_C4 is of the view that the institutions responsible for the educational system in Norway should address the needs of the companies to a greater extent. Students lack practical knowledge, and this is apparent within the firms. With regard to the bachelor's programme, progress has already been made in terms of establishing more practice-related learning units. Particularly in the age of renewable energies, the interview partner believes that relevance should be attached to not forgetting old technical knowledge and to continuing to include the corresponding content in the study programmes.

Outlook

Higher education qualifications in Norway have a high degree of value on paper and play a major role in the absence of any (private) contacts with companies. After completing his bachelor's degree, Oliver would like to work for a company where he can enter the area of production. Adrian would like to be appointed to a new (higher) position in the company for which he already worked prior to his programme of study.

View of the educational establishment

NO_EI_CS1 emphasises the high degree of motivation displayed by the *Y-veien* students compared to their fellow undergraduates. He believes that they are more mature and more experienced, and that their behaviour reveals that they are used to a company environment. Getting up early, working and learning in a planned way and a responsible attitude towards money are all nothing new for them.

Graduates of the *Y-veien* programme are in great demand on the labour market (NO_EI_CS1). The *Department of Electrical Engineers and Electricians* at the *Norwegian Trade Organisation* believes that there is a major need for skilled workers who understand the specific work situation on a construction site. Many skilled workers and engineers work at such locations. There is often conflict, misunderstanding and even distrust between the tradesmen and university-trained engineers who have never been on a building site before. However, someone in possession of both qualifications would be able to speak both languages. "But if the engineer has this trade certificate himself then they are speaking the same language" (68).

Conclusion

Students appreciate the *Y-veien* model of the bachelor's study programme and perceive it as an opportunity to gain broadly based higher academic and professional training. The challenges are certainly the question of financing after several years of occupational activity and the fact that students find themselves in a learning situation once more.

The company representatives interviewed appreciate the maturity and occupational experience of the *Y-veien* graduates and see them as an important link in everyday working life between skilled workers and university engineers. The graduates are familiar with both worlds and act as a type of mediator.

For the university college, the model has proved to be a success. Slight variations have been made to the programme in the intervening years since its initial pilot launch, and it is now also being offered by other institutes of higher education. Although the mix of students of different ages and with different life experiences and habits is a challenge, the way in which the two groups of students provide each other with mutual inspiration has been perceived as an enrichment. Because courses run in parallel in some instances, the organisational demands of the study programme are high.

Case study 2: Continuing vocational training programme at the technical college, i.e. fagskole

Overview of interviews

NO_ST_CS2	Students Elias and Svein*
NO_EI CS2_1	Technical college
NO_EI CS2_2	Teacher at the TC
NO_C2	Owner of an architectural firm which was established in 1997. He employs ten staff and is a qualified architect. From 1993 to 1995, he attended a technical college in order to learn a 3D programme.
NO_C3	Representative of a construction company association (EBA). The association represents the companies in the regions of Telemark, Buskerud and Vestfold.

*Names altered

Background information

The continuing training programmes at the *fagskole* encompass the areas of "Electro Topics", "Building & Construction" and "Production Technology". These continuing training measures are usually of a duration of two years. Participants use the programmes as an opportunity to pursue further training and gain a specialisation. However, approximately 60% of participants are in full-time employment. This means that they attend the programme on a part-time basis and complete it over a period of three years. Alongside technical programmes, continuing training programmes of a duration of one year are also offered in the field of nursing. A high proportion of the training is supported via web-based tools and digital media. The continuing training programmes are open to those who have completed upper secondary schooling or to persons in work with five years of relevant occupational experience. Within the scope of the European Qualifications Framework, the programme is aligned to Level 5.

The number of students at the *fagskole* has doubled over the past three years, and in the opinion of the interview partner (NO_EI CS2_1) will continue to grow. "So – but now we are growing very rapidly and we expect to grow farther into the, further into the, into the future" (4). Previously, class sizes were approximately 12 to 14. The figure today is 25. Approval is needed from NOKUT (Norwegian Agency for Quality Assurance in Education) for content changes and further development of the programmes as well as with regard to practical components.

According to information provided by the interview partner (NO_EI_CS2_1), discussions are also ongoing as to whether the government will assume responsibility for the colleges. Up until now, responsibility has rested with the individual districts in Norway. There are also plans to consolidate the colleges. At the moment, there are many individual locations spread across the country. The hope is that centralisation will achieve a higher level of demand at the locations and will reduce costs.

No integrated practical phases are stipulated in the programme forming the object of investigation. Indeed, participants are already in possession of several years of occupational experience. In effect, practice takes place upstream.

Evaluation focusing on the participant perspective

Elias and Svein are in their first year at the *technical college* in the area of "Building and Construction". There are 25 participants in their class, and the average age is around 32.

Access

Elias had already gained nine years of occupational experience prior to entering the programme. He was familiar with the course because his father had completed it 23 years previously. Svein has been working in the construction sector for 20 years and would like to use the measure to deepen his experience and gain a specialisation. The programme offers a choice of 20 specialist subject areas.

Programme of study and projects

During the continuing training programme, Elias and Svein have two projects per subject, which they work on in groups of four to five. The technical college offers a pool of topics from which students can make their selection. At the moment, for example, there is considerable provision in the field of renewable energies. Companies may also approach the technical college with ideas and problem descriptions, and the students are able to make use of these too (NO_EI CS2_1). The college has guidelines in place to support students with their projects.

Around eight weeks are allocated to each project. At the end of each year, a final examination takes place in two subjects in the form of projects. Both a group and an individual mark are awarded. These projects need to be carried out in cooperation with external partners (companies). Students are able to work on their final projects on site at the relevant companies. Examination tasks are scrutinised by experts from practice in respect of quality and current validity (NO_EI CS2_1).

View of the training institution

The teachers at the *technical colleges* have the task of maintaining contacts with the companies on a "day to day" basis (59). There is no general coordinator for this function.

In the view of NO_EI_CS2_1, consideration should be given to establishing more formal cooperation with local companies. His wish would be for the college to receive a greater insight into the work and organisation of the firms so as to ensure that programmes are better matched to regional requirements.

Those completing a programme at the *technical college* can receive a credit transfer of up to 60 credit points for entry to a *university college*. In many cases, the *university colleges* do not recognise the qualifications. One of the reasons for this is the competition which exists between the *technical colleges* and the *university colleges*. A joint programme is currently being developed by the *technical college* in conjunction with six further institutions. The aim is for this to gain full recognition for progression to further academic programmes.

The *technical colleges* require more resources in order to be able to expand its continuing vocational training programmes in a professional manner and pursue their further development. However, in the view of the interview partner, increasing academisation is creating a vacuum between the academic and vocational training programmes. For this reason, so-called "short-time studies" which are offered at institutes of higher education and relate to practice in the construction sector will become increasingly important in future.

Svein's and Elias's class also contains very young participants who have not yet gained occupational experience. Svein believes that it is difficult to create a link between theory and practice if no practice is as yet in place. In addition, younger students find it significantly more difficult to acquire companies for the individual projects because their age and lack of experience do not appeal to the firms concerned.

Satisfaction and outlook

Elias considers this school-based continuing training at the technical collage as a kind of job which he attends every day from 8.00 am to 3.00 pm because he is able to link what he has learned with the work he has done in previous years. This practical aspect was also crucial to Svein. The two students state that this practical relevance is lacking at other higher education institutions.

Svein's continuing training means that he is beginning to gain a better understanding of the administrative structures in the company where he works. Previously, he had very much acted in accordance with the motto of "you do what the boss tells you to do" (NO_ST_CS2, 15). Despite having several years of occupational experience in the sector, Svein and Elias did not expect the learning effect and mass of content to be so great in the first year. Another factor is that they perceive their teachers to be very competent. ("Well the teachers are brilliant, most of them.") (NO_ST_CS2, 29). This alleviates any anxiety about re-entering an educational establishment which may be experienced by someone who had difficulties at school. Basic mathematical knowledge from Years 7 and 8 is, for example, repeated with the participants so as to create the same status of knowledge for the entire learning group.

Svein and Elias would do this continuing training measure again and would also recommend it.

View of the company and of the association representative

The company has good connections with the *Fagskole* and offers practice placements. However, many of the students who have applied do not have any occupational experience in the sector and have been rejected for this reason. Nevertheless, the company is not averse to the idea of making projects available for the students' final thesis.

The company is happy to employ those who have completed programmes at the *Fagskole*. One of the reasons for this is that the director himself studied on just such a training course at a technical college. Secondly, experience has shown the interview partner that those completing the training are very well suited to the tasks performed by a company like his. The continuing training programmes strengthen background knowledge required to prepare architectural drawings or develop designs.

In the opinion of the association representative NO_C3, companies are prepared to do more to make it possible for students to pursue a combination of work and learning. However, they require the help of the schools and universities in this regard. The main aim of the association of construction companies is to facilitate access to higher VET in the building industry for those who are in possession of a vocational qualification. Close contact is in place with the Norwegian Ministry of Education, with which regular dialogue takes place in respect of aspects such as training programme structures and the proportion of practice phases involved.

Interaction with the branch of industry is also offered. Groups from educational establishments such as the technical college are able to undertake excursions to companies. By the same token, information events are also staged at schools. Lower and upper secondary school pupils are also afforded an opportunity to gain initial insights into the construction sector. The association also undertakes active PR work in order to demonstrate to parents that there are alternative pathways to the academic route.

Conclusion

These two-year continuing training programmes at the *fagskolee* are very much appreciated by the participants interviewed because they are able to build on the occupational experience they have already acquired and gain chances for advancement or a return to the labour market. This also means that their previous achievements are recognised and held in esteem. In the view of the educational establishment, this training pathway closes a qualification gap between those in employment who have completed initial vocational education and training and graduates of university training. Because of the rising numbers of students, this profile is likely to become even more important in future. A *white paper* issued by the Ministry of Education and Research in 2016 also sends out a signal at policy level regarding the relevance and further development of the *fagskole*. The intention is for these to be expanded and strengthened over the course of the coming years (NORWEGIAN MINISTRY OF EDUCATION AND RESEARCH 2016).

3.3.6   Poland

Case study 1: Two-year programme at the Learning Centre of New Technology

Overview of case study interviews

PL_St_CS1	Trainees Tomasz and Jarek*
PL_EI_CS1_2	Training institution
PL_C_CS1	Company

*Names altered

Background information

The *Advanced Training Centre for Modern Technologies* is a regional educational establishment for the continuing training of adults (minimum age 18) which was founded in 2007. It has numerous partnerships in place with both Polish companies and foreign firms which have branches in Poland (*Kształcenia Ustawicznego Nowoczesnych Technologii w Łodzi*) and it also cooperates with the Technical University of Lodz and the Lodz Centre for Teacher Training. It sees itself as a provider for those interested in pursuing further vocational training or who wish to pursue a professional career in a different and new specialist area of trade and industry in the region in order to train the skilled workers necessary to meet demand. There are similar educational establishments in various Polish cities. The educational establishment maintains several branches in the region. The selection criterion for the locations was the presence of companies which have a need for qualified skilled workers. These companies exert an influence on programme content and on provision in general. In overall terms, the approach adopted by the educational establishment is highly company-oriented.

The programme extends over a total period of three years. For two years, it includes a form of dual training which bears a close resemblance to the German dual system in the secondary sector. This is followed by an entirely company-based year, during which participants are integrated into the work process. The programme has been in existence since 2012 and leads to a formal vocational "technician qualification" (in the relevant specialist area). It has been developed by the Advanced Training Centre for Modern Technologies in close cooperation with local or regional companies. Alongside dual training programmes, it also offers modular versions of specialist training programmes in the field of technology in particular. Some of these are completed at the centre, apart from a few weeks of practical placement.

The starting point for this programme was in 2009, when the centre entered into a cooperation agreement with a company from Swabia. They worked together to develop a two-year programme aimed at private-sector technical occupations (engineering, electricians etc.). The apprentices have highly differing prior school learning. This ranges from full-time school-based vocational education and training in the secondary sector to a general upper secondary school leaving certificate providing a higher education entrance qualification. Apprentices spend three days a week at a company academy specially set up for the purpose and two days at the Training Centre, i.e. a branch of the centre in Lodz.

Learners receive a training allowance and are required in work at the company providing training for a certain period of time following completion of the programme. This payment rises from year to year. Because the programme has a modular structure, it is possible to combine training with employment (PL_EI_CS1_1).

Approximately 200 agreements are now in place with other companies to provide this type of dual training for young adults. These two-year programmes are unofficially viewed as qualifications at EQF Level 5. The programme was selected as the object for a case study because it constitutes a dual form of work-based learning at a higher educational level. One notable fact is that also higher education graduates complete such two-year programmes upon after having finished their academic studies in order to acquire practical skills in preparation for entry to the labour market. Someone graduating in journalism will, for example, take part in a programme on media and recording technology and films etc.

Evaluation focusing on the trainee perspective

Tomasz and Jarek are both in possession of a higher education entrance qualification.

Access

After completing his schooling and vocational education and training in the field of electronics, Jarek commenced a course in economics at a technical institute of higher education. However, he dropped out because he considered his studies to be pointless. He felt that there was a lack of practical relevance. He learned about the programme at the Advanced Training Centre from his brother, who had completed the same programme and now works for a German company and is based in both Poland and Germany.

Tomasz had no idea what to do next upon completing his schooling. He obtained a place at Częstochowa University, but had problems in financing his studies. He began to work, but lacked prospects. His grandmother told him about this dual programme available at the Training Centre, and he submitted an application. He is able to gain practical experience whilst undergoing vocational education and training. He also receives payment and will subsequently have good chances of obtaining a job. He feels that this is a great option for him, having never previously heard of this dual model. He is very happy and describes his decision to enter the programme as one of the best he has made in his life thus far.

Jarek lives in Lodz, where he submitted his application to the Training Centre. It was then forwarded to the company, which makes the decision on the selection of applicants. He has had to accept a daily commute since beginning his training. Tomasz applied to the company directly.

Theory and practice

Both students are currently in the second year of the "Mechatronics" programme and have concluded a training contract with the same company. The company is around 100 kilometres from Lodz. The Advanced Training Centre has a branch at the location, meaning that the two days at school and three days in the company/academy can take place at the same venue. At the time of the interview, around 160 trainees were completing this special training programme in this company. The company employs approximately 1,600 staff in Poland.

Tomasz explains that he was even a little anxious about the practice phase at the outset. He initially felt unsure about working with technical drawings in the company. It all seemed so new. But he quickly acquired a great deal of learning, and is now passionate about some of the technical tasks he performs in the company.

Both even find that they are able to make use of the technical skills they learn and acquire within their personal environment. Tomasz believes that the training has boosted his confidence, because he knows he will subsequently be able to get a job. This is also of major significance to Jarek, who on two occasions during the interview volunteers the opinion that he is now learning something which is useful and which will enable him to earn money. This is something which makes sense to him.

Jarek obtained the textbooks from his brother and approached the training and his time in the company with some degree of confidence. He did not feel like an outsider.

Learning in a work-related way via company experience and by using the machines and technical equipment is precisely the right approach for the two students. They are very positive in their remarks. Both find the variety of learning venues to be a great enrichment.

The school-based component of the programme is modular, and each module is followed by an examination. At the end of the second year, there is a practical examination in which they are required to produce a component or complete a technical drawing. When asked whether a contact in the company is available to them for the whole of the duration of the programme, Tomasz explains that each area has its own trainer.

View of the company

The company (PL_C_CS1), which is based in Germany and has a branch in Poland, developed the dual training programme in conjunction with the Advanced Training Centre. An "academy" was opened directly next to the works for this purpose. The company was motivated to take this step because it perceived a requirement for skilled workers with practical experience, something which in the experience of the interview partner the educational system in Poland is unable to provide. The academy acts as the company-based learning venue during training. It contains apprentice workshops and the same machinery which is used in production. Seven teachers work there. The curriculum has been jointly drawn up by the company, the Advanced Training Centre and representatives from the Polish Schools Ministry. The programme was first piloted in 2009. The interview partner was highly satisfied with the degree of influence which the company is able to exert on learning content.

According to the company, trainees are not deployed in the production process during the first two years of training. This takes place in the third year after the examinations have been completed. In the view of the interview partner, this removes pressure from the apprentices because quality, unit numbers and productivity are highly important. Neither those who have completed vocational education and training at secondary level nor higher education graduates would have the necessary and desired practical experience. By way of contrast, those completing practice-oriented training programmes enjoyed considerable potential for a professional career in the company.

The teaching staff at the academy are company practitioners. They have many years of experience and complete pedagogical training courses to prepare them for their teaching activities. The company organises additional German language courses alongside the school-based language instruction. This is very important to the company, and the teaching provided at the school is not sufficient in this regard.

One recurrent problem is that students leave for Germany or other companies in Poland upon completion of the programme. This tendency is, however, not too widespread. To his knowledge, other companies in Poland do not follow this model and take their lead from the commitment shown by his company. In fact, they are seeking to benefit by poaching staff. Neither are they in the financial position to fund comparable provision, e.g. by setting up an academy. Because the company itself has a great need for skilled workers which will increase sharply over the coming years, it does not offer cooperation arrangements to other firms in the form of offering use of the academy for a fee or embarking on joint training.

In order to receive a sufficient number of applications for the dual training programme, the company organised its first open day for school pupils in 2015. The interview partner, who is also the Head of Training, visits schools to talk about the training and the company. Each year, it becoming more difficult to find enough interested pupils. He believes that this is because too great a focus is placed on higher education study. Young school-leavers do not think about which occupation they wish to enter after completing their studies or about future plans. The main thing is to obtain a degree, any degree.

He estimates that around 10% of those who compete the training have a higher education qualification, but are still unable to find a job. The programme is also chosen by those who have already completed vocational education and training because they have not been able to gain any practical experience during such a course and also fail to find employment with the qualification they have acquired. Some applicants have trained in other occupations and are now seeking to move in a new professional direction.

This programme now constitutes the sole recruitment pathway for the company in respect of skilled workers. Selection decisions for the training programme are made by the company, although applications are also received via the Training Centre.

Jarek finds this dual form of training so positive because he is able to work with new machines and new tools in the company. At school, this was not the case. Another problem is that the specialist teaching materials and textbooks at school are out of date. During their second year of training, they also spent two weeks in the company in Germany.

Satisfaction and outlook

The students would definitely recommend this dual training programme. Tomasz also passed on this advice to his brother, who wished to start work with the company directly without prior training. He strongly believes that the training will enable him to find a job anywhere in Europe, but when he has completed the programme his aim is to pursue a career at the company which is providing his training. Like his brother, Jarek wishes to work for a company in Germany. He speaks very good German and was also able to conduct the interview in the language. He did not begin to learn German until he started the training programme. This is a notable "side effect" of the bi-national alignment of the training.

View of the educational establishment

For the Training Centre (PL_EI_CS1_2), the cooperation agreement it entered into with a Swabian company provided the initial spark for the development of the programme and for cooperation with further companies. The model also proved attractive for Polish companies, which has led them to display an increasing readiness to cooperate. The distrust that the sole focus was on financing the educational establishment gradually subsided. Because the educational establishment is also responsible for the quality of the company-based phases of learning, cooperation is based on a contractual agreement.

Although companies now articulate their skills needs, these are often couched in very general terms. The education institution then "translates" these requirements into relevant curricula or adapts existing training plans. One aim of the training centre is to expand the number of dual programmes, the number of participants and the number of cooperating companies. The training centre wishes to develop into a training provider which offers secondary school leavers direct subsequent access to a form of dual training.

The training centre will continue its efforts to create a closer link between training and the labour market in future. This is seen as being very important. The expectation is that educational policy will establish mechanisms and processes which facilitate this closer connection. In order for this to happen, incentives must be made available to companies to compensate them for the costs they incur as a result of their commitment.

From the point of view of the interview partner, the function of the School Director is that of a manager. Managers should be under a general obligation to report annually on their work and progress. External communication, e.g. with the companies, is very important. Unfortunately, this aspect is frequently neglected. Nevertheless, it takes time to make changes.

Cooperation with the companies is so important because schools cannot always afford to procure state-of-the-art technology and the latest equipment for their workshops and laboratories. For this reason, it is urgently necessary for learners to come into contact with such facilities when working in the company and to undergo training there.

In the view of the interview partner, advanced training centres should become more specialised and not, for example, offer the same foundation courses in mechatronics everywhere.

The interview partner also criticises the lack of a recognisable system at national level to identify labour market requirements.

He believes that it is fundamentally necessary for the policy level to send out stronger and clearer signals regarding the overall attractiveness and importance of vocational education and training and for more extensive reporting and communication to take place of the existing positive developments. Vocational education and training is still considered to be the poorest form of education.

Conclusion

The programme offered by the Advanced Training Centre closes a gap in the formal educational system, and this is made clear by the students in the interviews. In the tertiary sector in Poland, which is conterminous with the higher education sector, practice orientation and practical experience remain rare. This programme offers professional specialisation for graduates or an alternative dual course for adults which combines company-based and school-based training. Apprentices are paid and have good prospects of subsequent employment. The partner company influences training content and invests in its own training centre ("academy") in order to train suitable skilled workers. In this case too, the commitment of the parties involved, i.e. the education institution and the company, is crucial to the existence and attractiveness of the training programme and compensates for the lack of relevant formal provision in the education system.

The interview with the education institution makes it clear that the costs of the companies are not necessarily viewed as an investment in the future. There is also little perception of the benefits derived by the companies as a result of their commitment, such as perfectly matched skilled workers or productivity during the third year of the programme. The involvement of the companies in the development of training content and the training service itself are also considered from a cost perspective by the training provider. There is a desire for education policymakers to send out signals to the companies that their contribution is valued and to encourage greater commitment.

In overall terms, dual learning and close cooperation with regional trade and industry is held in very high esteem.

Case study 2: "Mechanical Engineering", at a state school of higher professional education (SSHPE)

Overview of interviews

PL_St_CS2	Filip and Piotr*
PL_EI_CS2	Representatives of the SSHPE
PL_C_CS2	Group interviews with representatives of four companies

*Names altered

Background information

The study programme is of four years' duration and combines academic with practice- oriented and applied learning. It leads to an *Inżynier* qualification, i.e. a bachelor's degree in engineering subjects. The education institution is a *state school of higher professional education (SSHPE)*, founded in 1998. In an international context, such institutions are referred to as *universities of applied sciences* and form part of the higher education sector in Poland. The term "university" may not, however, be used within the Polish context (PL_EI_CS2, 43). Numerous cooperation agreements are in place with companies in the region. The subject areas offered at the SSHPEs are technology, applied information technology, business studies, teacher training and languages.

Despite the relevance to the education system in Poland of the *state schools of higher vocational education (SSHVET)*, which fill a gap in the qualifications system thanks to their company proximity and alignment, it is not easy for them to compete with the university centres. The general reasons for this are the low degree of esteem accorded to vocational education in Poland and a sceptical and hostile attitude from within academic circles (Saryusz-Wolski et al. 2016). Demographic developments are also exacerbating the competitive situation between the training providers.

Local policymakers originally gave consideration to founding a university in the city where the SSHPE in the case study is located. But finally they were not, however, convinced of the merits of the idea. In overall terms, Poland has too few institutions in the higher education sector which are practice-oriented and focus on applied learning (PL_EI_CS2).

Around a fifth of students study on a part-time basis. (In 2013/14, total student numbers at the SSHPE were 2,880.) The SSHPE has a residential facility. The vast majority of students are from the closer and more distant region.

The subject area of "technology" is subdivided into various specialisms, and these are reviewed every five to seven years. Environmental technology and environmental protection were the last two new specialisms to be introduced. The development and requirements of the labour market are the crucial aspect. The most important basis is data supplied by the local employment agencies. German has been removed from the foreign languages subject area due to lack of interest.

Courses are also taught in company laboratories over the first three years of study, not merely during the practical phase. The third year of study is characterised by the carrying out of a practice-oriented project, which is coordinated and supported by a teacher from the company. This means that the programme is divided into two parts – a two-year component which tends to be theoretically oriented and a subsequent practice-related element. The aims of this combination are to avoid too close a focusing on one particular company and to ensure that those completing the programme enjoy greater flexibility on the labour market. The structure of the curricula is about to undergo a change which will now see professional competences defined as learning outcomes. The curricula will be structured in a modular way in future (PL_EI_CS2.)

The legal foundation of the SSHPE does not stipulate any extended practical placements. This provides a certain flexibility with regard to duration. Achieving the stipulated learning outcomes is the paramount objective. Numerous agreements have been concluded between the SSHPE and companies. These form the legal basis for the placements completed by the students. Students do not enter into any additional contract with the companies.

Senior lecturers with master's qualifications perform the teaching duties on the programme alongside professors, associate professors and lecturers holding doctorates. These senior lecturers also particularly include the company experts who teach at the SSHPE.

Evaluation focusing on the perspective of the students

Filip and Piotr are 23 and 22 years of age, respectively, both are in the fourth year of *Mechanical Engineering course.*

Access

Filip already has a technician qualification from the secondary sector. He has always been interested in machines and technology. Piotr is in possession of a general higher education entrance qualification.

Course of study and practice placement

The programme stipulates a four-month practical placement in the fourth year of study before the bachelor's thesis is completed in the final semester. The bachelor's thesis addresses issues which originate from the companies where students have done their placement. The bachelor's thesis is prepared during the placement.

At the time of the interview, both students were completing their practical phase at different companies in the region. The headquarters of Filip's firm is located in Switzerland. He had endeavoured to obtain a placement with this company because he wished to involve himself with gear systems. These machines are used in mines. He is currently deployed in an area which is responsible for production documentation. The application took place via the institute of higher education. Special application forms exist for this purpose.

Piotr is completing his practical placement in a major international company. The good reputation it enjoys was important for his selection. He hopes to obtain a job at this company after finishing his qualification. His aim in completing the placement here is to facilitate this step. His area of deployment is similar to that of Filip. Both have a contact/tutor in their company.

Satisfaction

Both students have the impression and the hope that this practice-oriented study programme will facilitate their transition to employment. They feel that they are being well prepared to enter working life. Piotr would like the programme to contain a larger proportion of technical subjects and practical placements, even in the initial semesters. His view is that there should be a greater number of practical exercises in overall terms, for example in the company laboratories with which he became familiar during his practice placement. He very much enjoyed this different learning environment and contact with the specific application of technology in the company.

View of the companies

The companies represented by the interview partners are regional SMEs which are primarily involved in technology, engineering and turbine construction.

They are represented on various advisory committees at the SSHPE, including on the Mechanical Engineering Committee in the Technology Department. Such discussions are very important in terms of ensuring that the learning outcomes of the programmes are compatible with the needs of the companies. Meetings focus on aspects such as structuring of the practice phases, any new content areas which may be required and topics for theses. They are held two or three times a year. Employees from the companies represented also act as teaching staff at the SSHPE.

A contractual agreement is in place between the companies and the SSHPE which governs cooperation with practice placements, the issue of awarding placements and the bachelor's projects. Some of these agreements have been in existence for many years.

As well as having professional connections with the SSHPE, one interview partner also has a personal link to the institution as his son also studies there. He actually graduated in the same building, although the institute was still a branch of the Technical University of Gdańsk at the time. This shows the regional networking and relevance of the SSHPEs.

Speaking about the topic of the bachelor's thesis, one company interview partner remarks that the firms view these as an opportunity for students to get to grips with a current topic.

The companies also believe that the practice phases are useful to them because they are able to get to know the students much better than is possible in three- or four-hour interviews. Longer observation is necessary because *soft skills* are particularly important. This also means that the practice phase serves as a recruitment instrument for the companies. In the case stated above, approximately 50% of the students who do a placement are offered permanent employment after achieving their qualification.

By the same token, the students also perceive the practice phase as being useful because they are able to gain an insight into the company and its production methods. They experience in highly specific terms what it means to work as part of a team and to adopt a wholly practical approach to problem-solving. They have the chance to apply or test out their theoretical knowledge in practice. In the experience of one interview partner, the students display greater confidence after the placement. "As far as we know after this kind of internship the student is much more brave, courageous and has the skill to actually come up with problems and look for solutions because this university gives a certain basic knowledge and when working in the company they have the possibility to check their work" (109).

Students do not receive payment during the practice placement.

The experience of the interview partners from the companies is that company-based teachers sometimes acquire students for practice placements from their own firms. In other cases, however, students apply directly. One interview partner bemoans the fact that students prefer to complete their placements at larger companies which communicate their needs directly to the SSHPE.

The companies have selected "*certified*" tutors to provide support to students during the practice phases. A company may, for example, have an average of 20 students per year and appoint 17 tutors. Tutors are members of staff who assume this function in addition to their professional tasks.

They also recruit graduates from institutes of higher education such as the Technical University of Gdańsk. Their experience is that SSHPE graduates are significantly better prepared for their occupational tasks in comparison. A further interview partner states that his company primarily recruits those completing the SSHPE programme as engineers.

A look at future developments and challenges

The SSHPE forming the object of the case study is part of a major national EU-funded project which aims to lead to an expansion of practice placements at the state schools. One particular objective is to extend the duration of practice placements to six months and to implement a mandatory placement of several months at the other SSHPEs for the first time. Support for the achievement of this goal is being provided by the Ministry of Research and Higher Education.

The interviews highlight the high degree of significance accorded to the imparting of soft skills alongside professional and technical competences. The aim is to ensure "holistic education" (277) in the broadest sense of the term rather than merely teaching narrowly defined company-oriented professional competences. Considerable importance is also attached to sport as a way of teaching fair play, sport teaches theatre etc.

From the point of view of the interview partner, companies require qualified skilled workers below the engineer or bachelor's level. For this reason, he believes that it is very important to undertake projects which develop curricula at EQF Level 5 in the area of IT. These are currently absent in Poland. This would also act as an instrument for those who drop out of a bachelor's programme. It may be possible for such students to obtain a relevant credit transfer for skills gained and thus to acquire a qualification. Because this topic is still very much in its infancy, it is still also unclear whether such two-year programmes could be integrated into the higher education sector or aligned to the area of vocational education and training. Their SSHPE would be able to implement programmes of this nature.

The interview partners from the companies remark that keeping up with the pace of technological changes in the firms represents a major challenge for the educational system. In the view of one interview partner, *soft skills* once again have a central part to play in this regard. They enable students to adapt to a new technological work environment quickly and provide the ability to cope with new challenges. The development of the competence of *learning to learn* should be particularly fostered by the institutes of higher education. This also includes learning how to use sources such as the Internet. Another consideration was whether to support the idea that theses should be written in English in future. Three interview partners believe that it is extremely important to expand foreign language skills.

According to one interview partner, the future development of the practice placements and the amount of commitment which can be shown going forward depend on the economic performance of the company. He currently remains optimistic and would like to offer more places.

Conclusion

How companies in the region are involved and the extent to which they are able to integrate practice phases into the curriculum depends heavily on the initiative shown by the individual institute of higher education. The SSHPE forming the object of investigation here is certainly a shining example of how success can be achieved with such an approach. The students appreciate the practical relevance of the programme and the opportunity to gain experience. They believe that this offers them advantages when they seek to secure a job after obtaining their qualification. Companies are involved via teaching input from their staff, via the support provided to students by tutors during the practice phases and via agreement of the topics for the bachelor's thesis. They also participate in committees which consult on new courses of study or the updating of existing programmes and accord due consideration to the companies' point of view. The companies view the practice placement as part of their human resources acquisition strategy.

3.4   Summary

There are approaches to forms of WBL or of higher vocational education and training programmes in the tertiary sector in all six countries investigated.

Structures and organisation are not uniform because the characteristics of the respective tertiary educational sector follow the differing structures of the various secondary education systems, which in turn have their basis in different traditions. Academic education is held in similarly high esteem in all of the countries, although the non-academic area of tertiary education bears highly distinctive hallmarks in each case. The content of current educational policy debate thus varies accordingly, and individually matched approaches are being considered in respect of the future developments of WBL in the tertiary educational sector.

▶ The introduction of *higher* and *degree apprenticeships* in England represents an attempt to diversify the higher education sector and to introduce a more practice-oriented element to *mass higher education.*[55]

▶ In Ireland, new *apprenticeships* are also being created in the tertiary sector.

▶ Poland is undertaking initial attempts to improve the attractiveness of vocationally-oriented and practice-related tertiary education by expanding *SSHVET* so as to establish an alternative to conventional university-based bachelor's study programmes.

▶ Norway is currently going down the route of enriching higher education study programmes by adding practical placements and is also seeking to strengthen the vocational colleges. At the same time, an innovative approach is being developed in some subject areas to access to bachelor's programmes for those with vocational qualifications. The competences already acquired by such persons are taken into account, and they are able to join their counterparts with general upper secondary school leaving qualifications to study for a joint bachelor's degree. This additional permeability may exert a positive effect on the attractiveness of vocational education and training in the secondary sector.

▶ Practice-oriented higher education study programmes have been in place in France for many years, and a considerable proportion of these may be completed in the form of *apprentissages*.

▶ Initial dual programmes of higher education study have emerged in Austria over recent years. Advanced vocational training has traditionally played a comparatively large role alongside higher education, even though it is classified as being non-formal and does not therefore constitute a formal part of the educational system which is statistically recorded. The WKÖ in particular is undertaking considerable endeavours to make this educational pathway more attractive by according recognition to the qualifications or by ensuring that they lead to a qualification which has an equivalence in the formal educational sector. The chambers and the professional associations are the principal stakeholders in this regard. Although Norway, France and Poland also have comparable continuing vocational training opportunities, these are restricted to certain occupations, frequently in the craft trades sector. They are relatively low in number and do not form a topic which is being addressed by education and training stakeholders.

---

55 A similar approach is currently being piloted in Australia, where the existing *traineeships* in the tertiary educational sector are being turned into *apprenticeships*. Unlike in England, however, these are aligned to the VET sector and can be offered by TAFEs and other registered training providers.

Dual study programmes

While France is able to look back on a long tradition of *apprentissages* in the tertiary sector, *apprenticeships* in England and Ireland represent targeted educational policy activities that aim to strengthen or establish tertiary sector programmes which correspond to forms of dual training or dual programmes of higher education study. Dual study programmes have also been created in Austria. By way of contrast, comparable dual structures in the tertiary educational sector have not been introduced in Poland and Norway.

The *role of the companies* in the programmes forming the object of investigation also varies considerably. Programmes such as the training-integrated and practice-integrated dual courses of study in Germany feature a close interlinking between institutes of higher education with regard to the various levels of cooperation, for example collaboration governed by contractual agreement, joint development of coordinated programme content, (partial) financing of institutions by companies. Apart from the last point, a similar link exists in respect of dual programmes of study in Austria, where learning phases at the institute of higher education and in the company are also clearly regulated and coordinated. In France, on the other hand, cooperation in respect of *apprentissages* in the BTS, DUT and LP programmes is less extensive. These phases are regulated in terms of time, but otherwise largely run in parallel and independently. Although informal cooperation agreements are in place in individual cases, these are not the object of contractual regulation. The stakeholders have the greatest degree of flexibility in respect of structuring learning content in the LP programmes, and this means that account can be taken of the skills requirements of the companies in the region.

In England, the linking of learning during the programme of study and at work primarily takes place via study projects conducted in the workplace. The "Electrical Apprenticeship" in Ireland constitutes an exception in this regard because it is a formal dual training programme which provides employers with specific stipulations for work-based learning.

Forms and functions of WBL in the tertiary educational sector

Typification of forms of WBL programmes with regard to specific criteria such as duration of the company-based phases, organisation, role of the companies, status of the students or similar aspects does not lead to any deeper findings because a far too dominant role is exercised by the significance of the overall structure of the educational system and the characteristics and importance of vocational education and training. Characteristics are also highly dependent on the general local conditions governing education and training programmes. Nevertheless, the literature analysed and interviews conducted within the scope of the project make it clear that growing significance is being attached to work-based, practice-oriented learning in the tertiary educational sector.

With regard to the function of the work-based programmes, a distinction can be drawn between four types. These are, however, frequently found in a combined form and are mostly not the sole definers of the character of the programmes.

Table 2: Summary of functions

"Extension" function	Within the scope of this function, academic programmes are extended with regard to content alignment by WBL in the form of practical placements or via the integration of formalised vocational learning (e.g. dual first programmes of study in Germany).
Upskilling/professionalisation/ specialisation function	These programmes focus on specialisation, consolidation or widening of existing professional competences, e.g. advanced vocational training.
"Bridging" function	Programmes with this function have the aim of facilitating permeability (in particular of secondary vocational training) to higher education or academic programmes of study.
Tertiary "High–level" IVET/PET	Programmes which offer initial vocational education and training in the higher education sector[56] (e.g. BTS, DUT in France, degree apprenticeships in England).

If we transfer these functional categories to the 12 programmes investigated, we arrive at the following very rough alignment.

---

56   As opposed to the "extension function", where secondary vocational education and training may, for example, be integrated into a higher education programme.

Table 3: Alignment of the programmes investigated to the functions

	"Extension" function	Upskilling/professionalisation/ specialisation function	"Bridging" function	Tertiary high-level IVET
AT	Dual bachelor's study programme	Higher vocational qualification (Public Accountant)		Dual bachelor's study programme
EN	Foundation degree programme "Electrical and Electronic Engineering Programme" (for Higher Apprentices) Bachelor's degree Programme "WMG Applied Engineering Programme" (for Higher Apprentices)	Foundation degree programme "Electrical and Electronic Engineering Programme" (for sponsored students/some Higher Apprentices with vocational qualifications) Bachelor's degree programme "WMG Applied Engineering Programme" (for sponsored students/Higher Apprentices with a vocational qualification)	Foundation degree programme "Electrical and Electronic Engineering Programme" (for participants without A levels) Bachelor's degree programme "WMG Applied Engineering Programme" (some Higher Apprentices with a vocational qualification)	Foundation degree programme "Electrical and Electronic Engineering Programme" (for Higher Apprentices with A level)
F	Apprentissages in BTS, DUT/LP		Brevet de Technicien Supérieur (BTS)	Diplôme Universitaire de Technologie (DUT) and Licence professionelle (LP) Brevet de Technicien Supérieur (BTS)
IR	Higher Certificate "Information Technology Support Programme"		Higher Certificate "Information Technology Support Programme" (partially, because low entry hurdle for persons with vocational qualifications and for more mature applicants)	Advanced Certificate "Electrical Apprenticeship" (Further Education and Training) Higher Certificate "Information Technology Support Programme" (Higher Education)
NO		Programme at Technical College "Building and Construction"	Bachelor's programme "Y-Way" "Electrical Power Engineering"	
PL				State School of Higher Professional Education Two+one-year programme

This does not, however, produce a system in which certain forms can be aligned to certain functions. The tables simply allow a summary of the programmes and their functions to be presented.

4 Conclusion

Against the background of the theory propounded by Trow (see above), the present project makes a contribution towards the further differentiation of the higher education sector although the area of investigation also encompasses the non-higher education tertiary sector.

It has been possible to identify a strengthening and compaction of vocational education and training, i.e. work-based learning elements in the tertiary sector. In some cases, new qualifications are being introduced (*degree apprenticeships* in England and *new apprenticeships* in Ireland). Newly structured higher education programmes are also emerging (dual programmes of study in Austria), or relevant institutions are being strengthened (*vocational colleges* in Norway and the SSHVET in Poland). However, developments are heterogeneous in nature and do not follow a uniform formal pattern. This is a contributory factor to the circumstance that they are scarcely visible in the available quantitative data and in international educational statistics.

The observation of the emergence of new differentiation characteristics is also in line with the analyses of Arum et al. (2007).[57] Expansion of an educational sector or sub-sector of the type which has occurred in the area of higher education over the last few decades leads to qualitative internal differentiation (Arum et al. p. 4). A similar approach originates from organisation theory. The growth of an organisation is accompanied by differentiations (Blau 1970). When systems grow, they become more complex and new differentiations and internal structures arise.[58]

No indications could be identified that the vocational pathway in the higher education sector is a refuge or repository of lower status with the function of reserving higher status programmes for elite groups (Arum et al. 2007). The prestige these programmes in the tertiary sector enjoy compared to vocational education and training in the secondary sector is actually very high. This is particularly noticeable in England and France. The case studies suggest that the attitude of the companies is one of the reasons for this. They use the hybrid or dual programmes as a recruitment instrument. By the same token, this also means that students expect that access to such courses will bring the security of appropriate subsequent employment. The fact that the students are older and their greater level of maturity are of further benefit for the companies. This makes integration into the productive work process easier.

The companies therefore make high performance demands with regard to later recruitment of those completing the qualifications as young skilled workers and in respect of their expected "return on investment". These demands relate to marks achieved in prior educational qualifications and to company considerations in respect of which aspects such as social competences may play a major role. After demonstration of professional competence, competencies such as communication skills, the ability to act as a team player and commitment are crucial to the human resources selection procedure (Hippach-Schneider et al. 2013). To this extent, the selection process which takes place is fundamentally different to the admission procedures for institutes of higher education. The latter are frequently standardised and sometimes set out certain school performance requirements in the form of marks achieved.

---

57   This theoretical background opened up further during the course of the project.

58   At the same time, however, further differentiation may also lead to further expansion. One example of this is the universities of applied sciences in Germany. Provision such as dual programmes of study mean that they have represented an engine for growth in the higher education sector over recent years (Vocational Education and Training Reporting Authors' Group 2016).

Students are also seen as "mediators" of innovation and technology, which they bring to the company from the institutes of higher education. The benefit for the companies thus differs considerably from that provided by work-based learning programmes in the secondary sector. In the tertiary sector, WBL programmes are an attractive model for companies. Although students enjoy advantages such as payment and good prospects of appropriate employment, programmes often involve considerable time demand and require a marked sense of motivation.

The results of the project support the differentiation theory. However, differentiation is not primarily being reflected by the instigation of new educational establishments. A new differentiation is in fact taking place at the level of the programmes and in terms of the introduction of new qualifications or the *upgrading* of institutions. New educational administration bodies have emerged in some individual cases, including the *Apprenticeship Council* in Ireland and England's *Institute for Apprenticeships*. However, in terms of their structural significance and ability to bring about a sustainable change in governance practices, these developments do not correspond with the formation of new types of educational establishments (such as the universities of cooperative education in Germany in the 1970s) or the introduction of new national education and training courses (for example the BTS and DUT in France).

Differentiation is revealed via a specific linking of theoretical and practical learning at two learning venues or in relation to the selection and therefore the composition of students.

The area of advanced vocational education and training in the countries investigated faces the challenge that it is not perceived as part of the educational system. This means that it is scarcely visible internationally because it is inadequately mapped in international educational statistics. It would be desirable if these attractive forms of higher vocational education and training could be removed from the educational policy twilight zone. This is a particular challenge for Germany given the high degree of attractiveness which higher vocational education and training has previously enjoyed. One possible short-term solution to providing improved visibility could be the creation of internationally connective terminology for the whole sector with relevant designations for the certificates and qualifications. Germany will also see a rise in the proportion of companies which are internationally managed and act at a global level. These companies do not have links with the German qualifications system, which stretches back for many years. The value of the vocational pathway should be made clearer and more comprehensible to them in overall terms.

Annex/bibliography

ARUM, Richard; GAMORAN, Adam; SHAVIT, Yossi: More inclusion than diversion: expansion, differentiation, and market structure in higher education. In: SHAVIT, Yossi; ARUM, Richard; GAMORAN, Adam (eds): Stratification in higher education. Stanford, California 2007, pp. 1–35

AUTORENGRUPPE BILDUNGSBERICHTERSTATTUNG: Bildung in Deutschland 2016. Bielefeld 2016

CEDEFOP: Glossary – Quality in education and training 2011. – URL: http://www.cedefop.europa.eu/en/publications-and-resources/publications/4106 (Access: 11.04.2018)

CHARRAUD, Anne-Marie: Case Study on Higher Vocational Education and Training at EQF-Levels 5 to 7 in France. In: HIPPACH-SCHNEIDER, Ute; SCHNEIDER, Verena (Eds.): Tertiäre berufliche Bildung in Europa – Beispiele aus sechs Bildungssystemen. Bonn 2016, pp. 76–121

DEARING REPORT: Higher education in the learning society. Leeds 1997

DEPARTMENT FOR BUSINESS INNOVATION AND SKILLS: Progression of Apprentices to Higher Education – Cohort Update 2015. – URL: https://www.gov.uk/government/uploads/system/uploads/attachment_data/file/310028/bis-14-795-progression-of-apprentices-to-highe-education-cohort-update.pdf (Access: 11.04.2018)

DEPARTMENT FOR EDUCATION: Participation Rates In Higher Education: Academic Years 2006/2007–2015/2016 (Provisional) SFR 47/2017. London 2017 – URL: https://www.gov.uk/government/uploads/system/uploads/attachment_data/file/648165/HEIPR_PUBLICATION_2015-16.pdf (Access: 11.04.2018)

DEPARTMENT FOR EDUCATION AND SKILLS: Foundation Degrees: a consultation document. London 2000.

DEPARTMENT OF EDUCATION AND SKILLS: Ireland's National Skills Strategy 2025. Dublin 2016 – URL: https://www.education.ie/en/Publications/Policy-Reports/pub_national_skills_strategy_2025.pdf (Access: 11.04.2018)

DEPARTMENT OF EDUCATION AND SKILLS: Action Plan to expand Apprenticeship and Traineeship in Ireland 2016–2020. Dublin 2017 – URL: https://www.education.ie/en/Publications/Policy-Reports/Action-Plan-Expand-Apprenticeship-Traineeship-in-Ireland-2016-2020.pdf (Access: 11.04.2018)

GALLACHER, Jim; INGRAM, Robert; REEVE, Fiona: Work-based and work-related learning in Higher National Certificates and Diplomas in Scotland and Foundation Degrees in England: A Comparative Study: Final Report. Glasgow 2009

GIRET, Jean-Francois: Does Vocational Training Help Transition to Work? The 'New French Vocational Bachelor Degree'. In: European Journal of Education, 46 (2011) 2, part 2, p. 13

GRUBER, Benjamin; SCHMID, Kurt; NOWAK, Sabine: Evaluierung der Berufsakademie, Wien 2015

HIGHER EDUCATION STATISTICS AGENCY: Higher education undergraduate student enrolments and qualifications obtained at higher education providers in England 2015/16. Cheltenham 2017 – URL: https://www.hesa.ac.uk/news/08-02-2017/sfr244-ap-student-enrolments-and-qualifications (Access: 11.04.2018)

HIPPACH-SCHNEIDER, Ute: Akademisierung oder „vocational drift"? Internationale Entwicklungen im tertiären Bildungsbereich. In: Berufsbildung in Wissenschaft und Praxis 3 (2014), pp. 27–29

HIPPACH-SCHNEIDER, Ute: Tertiäre internationale Bildungsstatistik qualitativ interpretiert. In: SCHLÖGL, Peter et al. (eds): Berufsbildung – eine Renaissance. Bielefeld 2017, pp. 324–331

HIPPACH-SCHNEIDER, Ute; SCHNEIDER, Verena: Tertiäre berufliche Bildung in Europa – Beispiele aus sechs Bildungssystemen. Wissenschaftliche Diskussionspapiere 175. Bonn 2016

HIPPACH-SCHNEIDER, Ute et al.: The underestimated relevance and value of vocational education in tertiary education – making the invisible visible. In: Journal of Vocational Education and Training 69 (2017) 1, pp. 28–46

HIPPACH-SCHNEIDER, Ute et al.: Are graduates preferred to those completing initial vocational education and training? Case studies on company recruitment strategies in Germany, England and Switzerland. In: Journal of Vocational Education & Training 65 (2013), pp. 1–17

KUCKARTZ, Udo: Qualitative Inhaltsanalyse: Methoden, Praxis, Computerunterstützung. Weinheim 2014

LESTER, Stan: Higher Vocational Education and Training in England. In: HIPPACH-SCHNEIDER, Ute; SCHNEIDER, Verena (eds): Tertiäre berufliche Bildung in Europa – Beispiele aus sechs Bildungssystemen. Bonn 2016, pp. 44–75

MINISTÈRE DE L'ÉDUCATION NATIONALE DE L'ENSEIGNEMENT SUPÉRIEUR ET DE LA RECHERCHE (MENESR): L'état de l'Enseignement supérieur et de la Recherche en France – 50 indicateurs 2016. – URL: http://publication.enseignementsup-recherche.gouv.fr/eesr/9/EESR9_ES_11-le_profil_des_nouveaux_bacheliers_entrant_dans_les_principales_filieres_du_superieur.php (Access: 11.04.2018)

MINISTÈRE DE L'ÉDUCATION NATIONALE DE L'ENSEIGNEMENT SUPÉRIEUR ET DE LA RECHERCHE (MENESR): Higher Education and Research, Facts and Figures 2017. – URL: https://publication.enseignementsup-recherche.gouv.fr/eesr/9EN/source-MENESR_DEPP.php (Access: 11.04.2018)

NORWEGIAN MINISTRY OF EDUCATION AND RESEARCH: Skilled Workers for the Future: Vocational college education – an important part of the knowledge society: Policy background and summary. Report to the Storting (white paper). 2016–2017. Oslo 2016

NOU: Tertiary vocational colleges – an attractive education choice : Study by the Commission appointed by Royal Degree on 23 August 2013: submitted to the Ministry of Education and Research on 15 December 2014. Norges offentlige utredninger NOU. 2014. Oslo 2014

POWELL, Andrew: Apprenticeship Statistics: England. Briefing Paper Number 06113. 2018. – URL: http://researchbriefings.files.parliament.uk/documents/SN06113/SN06113.pdf

PULLEN, Charlynne; CLIFTON, Jonathan: England's Apprenticeships: assessing the new system. London 2016. – URL: https://www.ippr.org/files/publications/pdf/Englands_apprenticeships_Aug%202016.pdf (Access: 11.04.2018)

SARYUSZ-WOLSKI, Tomasz; PIETROWSKA, Dorota; OLEJNIK, Joanna: Case Study on Higher Vocational Education and Training at EQF-Levels 5 to 7 in Poland. In: HIPPACH-SCHNEIDER, Ute; SCHNEIDER, Verena (eds): Tertiäre berufliche Bildung in Europa – Beispiele aus sechs Bildungssystemen Bonn 2016, pp. 212–243

SOLAS: Apprenticeships.ie 2017: List of Apprenticeships. Dublin 2017– URL: http://www.apprenticeship.ie/en/apprentice/Shared%20Documents/List%20of%20Apprenticeships%20in%20Ireland.pdf (Access: 11.04.2018)

TEICHLER, Ulrich: Hochschulsysteme und quantitativ-strukturelle Hochschulpolitik. Münster, New York 2014

TROW, Martin: Problems in the transition from elite to mass higher education. Berkeley 1973

Trow, Martin: From mass higher education to universal access: The American advantage. Research and occasional paper series: CSHE Berkeley, California 2000

Trow, Martin: Reflections on the transition from elite to mass to universal access: forms and phrases of higher education in modern societies since WW II. Working Papers. Berkeley, California 2005 – URL: http://escholarship.org/uc/item/96p3s213 (Access: 11.04.2018)

Universities UK: Degree apprenticeships: realising opportunities. London 2017 – URL: http://www.universitiesuk.ac.uk/policy-and-analysis/reports/Pages/degree-apprenticeships-realising-opportunities.aspx (Access: 11.04.2018)

Vincens, Jean: Graduates and the Labour Market in France. In: European Journal of Education 30 (1995) 2, pp. 133–156

Wolf, Alison; Dominguez-Raig, Gerard; Sellen, Peter: Remaking Tertiary Education: can we create a system that is fair and fit for purpose? London 2016

Index of abbreviations

Abbreviation	Meaning
BBH	Bilanzbuchhaltungsbehörde (Accountancy Authority) (AT)
BacGen	Baccalauréat général (FR)
BacPro	Baccalauréat professionnel (FR)
BacTec	Baccalauréat technologique (FR)
bfi	Berufsförderungsinstitut (Vocational Training Institute) (AT)
BTS	Brévet de Technicien Supérieur (FR)
CAO	Central Applications Office (IE)
CPC	Commissions Professionelles Consultatives (FR)
DUT	Diplôme Universitaire de Technologie (FR)
EQF	European Qualifications Framework
Eurostat	Statistical Office of the European Union
FD	Foundation Degrees (EN)
FE	Further Education (EN and IE)
FH	Fachhochschule (University of Applied Sciences) (AT)
HE	Higher education
HEA	Higher Education Authority (IE)
HNC	Higher National Certificate (EN)
HND	Higher National Diploma (EN)
IfA	Institute for Apprenticeships (EN)
IoT	Institute of Technology (IE)
ISCED	International Standard Classification of Education
IUT	Instituts Universitaires de Technologie (FR)
LP	Licence professionelle (FR)
MEDEF	French employers' organisation
MENESR	Ministère de l'Éducation nationale de l'Enseignement supérieur et de la Recherche (FR)
MINT	German acronym for Mathematics, IT, Science, Technology (equivalent of STEM)
NFQ	National Framework of Qualifications (IE)
NGO	Non-governmental organisation
NOKUT	Norwegian Agency for Quality Assurance in Education (NO)
QQI	Quality and Qualifications Ireland (IE)
SMEs	Small and medium-sized enterprises
SOLAS	Irish Further Education and Training Authority
SSHPE	State School of Higher Professional Education (PL)
SSHVET	State School of Higher Vocational Education (PL)
STEM	Science, Technology, Engineering, Mathematics

WBL	Work-based learning
WIFI	Continuing training academy of the WKÖ (AT)
WKÖ	Association of Austrian Chambers of Commerce and Industry (AT)
WKW	Vienna Chamber of Commerce and Industry (AT)

Authors

Ute-Hippach Schneider

Academic researcher and Project Head of the "VET Systems in International Comparative Terms, Research and Monitoring" Division at the Federal Institute for Vocational Education and Training (BIBB)

Verena Schneider

Academic researcher in the "Electrical, IT and Scientific Occupations" Division at the Federal Institute for Vocational Education and Training (BIBB)

Abstract

Die Implementierung von arbeitsbasierten Lernphasen, sog. Work-based Learning, in Programme des tertiären Bildungsbereichs kann in seinen unterschiedlichen Ausprägungen und Konkretisierungen als ein Trend der letzten Jahre bezeichnet werden. Beispiele, die im Rahmen eines BIBB-Forschungsprojektes in England, Frankreich, Irland, Norwegen, Österreich und Polen untersucht worden sind, geben einen Einblick in die Vielfalt praxisorientierter und praxisintegrierter Bildungsprogramme im tertiären Bildungsbereich. In Interviews mit Vertreterinnen und Vertretern aus den Bereichen Forschung, Bildungspolitik, aber auch mit Studierenden, Betrieben und Bildungseinrichtungen werden konkrete Erfahrungen und Einschätzungen mit ausgewählten Bildungsprogrammen gewonnen. Insgesamt wollen das Projekt und diese Publikation einen Beitrag zu einer verbesserten Sichtbarkeit der beruflichen Bildung im tertiären Bildungsbereich beitragen und eine kritischere Auseinandersetzung mit der Frage nach einem Akademisierungstrend erleichtern.

The implementation of work-based learning elements in programmes of tertiary education can be seen as a trend of the last years. Different models and approaches have been developed. In the context of a BIBB research project, examples in England, France, Ireland, Norway, Austria and Poland were investigated, analysed and thus the great variety of practice-oriented and practice-integrated programmes disclosed. Interviews with representatives from research, education policy administration but also with students, companies and education institutions provide an insight into concrete experience and appraisal of selected education programmes. Overall, the project as well as this publication aim to contribute to a better visibility of vocational/professional education at tertiary level and facilitate a more critical debate about the issue of an increasing academisation.

GPSR Authorized Representative: Easy Access System Europe, Mustamäe tee
50, 10621 Tallinn, Estonia, gpsr.requests@easproject.com

www.ingramcontent.com/pod-product-compliance
Lightning Source LLC
Chambersburg PA
CBHW080853120626
46550CB00008B/2628